Public Opinion in America and Japan

Public Opinion in America and Japan

How We See Each Other and Ourselves

Everett Carll Ladd and
Karlyn H. Bowman

The AEI Press

Publisher for the American Enterprise Institute
Washington, D.C.

The Roper Center for Public Opinion Research
University of Connecticut
Storrs, Connecticut

1996

This monograph is a joint research project and publication of the American Enterprise Institute for Public Policy Research, Washington, D.C., and the Roper Center for Public Opinion Research, University of Connecticut, Storrs, Connecticut.

Available in the United States from the AEI Press, c/o Publisher Resources Inc., 1224 Heil Quaker Blvd., P.O. Box 7001, La Vergne, TN 37086-7001. Distributed outside the U.S. by arrangement with Eurospan, 3 Henrietta Street, London WC2E 8LU England.

Library of Congress Cataloging-in-Publication Data

Ladd, Everett Carll.

     Public opinion in America and Japan : how we see each other and our-
selves / Everett Carll Ladd and Karlyn H. Bowman.

       p. cm.

     Includes bibliographical references.

     ISBN 0-8447-7057-4 (alk. paper).

     1. Public opinion—United States. 2. Public opinion—Japan. 3. United
States—Relations—Japan—Public opinion. 4. Japan—Relations—
United States—Public opinion. 5. United States—Foreign public opin-
ion, Japanese. 6. Japan—Foreign public opinion, American.   I.
Bowman, Karlyn H. II. Title.

HN90.P8L33 1996

303.3'8'0973—dc20

96–7381
CIP

1 2 3 4 5 6 7 8 9 10

THE AEI PRESS
Publisher for the American Enterprise Institute
1150 Seventeenth Street, N.W.
Washington, D.C. 20036

Printed in the United States of America

In this and like communities, public sentiment is every-thing. With public sentiment, nothing can fail; without it nothing can succeed. Consequently he who moulds public sentiment, goes deeper than he who enacts statutes or pronounces decisions. He makes statutes and decisions possible or impossible to be executed.

—ABRAHAM LINCOLN
First Debate, at Ottawa, Illinois
August 21, 1858

Contents

Preface

Book authors go through certain rituals. In particular, they acknowledge that they are not infallible and accept responsibility for any error they may inadvertently have committed. And they express thanks to colleagues, friends, family members, and others who helped make completion of the book possible.

We have special and intense reasons both to wish and to need to make such acknowledgments. The always present fact of author fallibility is extended here, because neither of us is a student of Japanese society or politics. This underscored, we have had some expert coaching, and we bring broad experience in survey research and in the interpretation of public opinion information. As to the debt we owe others—it is wide and deep. Far more than most books and certainly more than any book either of us has been involved with previously, this is a collective effort. It is a pity that the term *team effort* has come to sound so banal, because this book is truly a team effort.

We are delighted to acknowledge the financial support of the Center for Global Partnership (CGP) of the Japan Foundation, and in particular the continuing encouragement given to us by Yoo Fukazawa, director of the CGP. It was a grant made in 1992 by the CGP to the Roper Center that put in motion the archive-building efforts that made this volume possible.

A host of survey organizations have generously made their data available to the Roper Center, permitting a broad comparative collection on the United States and Japan to emerge. In particular, we want to acknowledge the outstanding survey research and the generosity of the *Asahi Shimbun,* CBS News, Dentsu, Inc., the Gallup Organization, the International Social Survey Programme, the Jiji Press, Louis Harris and Associates, the National Opinion Research Center, the *New York Times,* the *Nihon Keizai Shimbun,* Nippon Hoso Kyokai (NHK), the Prime Minister's Office in Japan, Roper Starch

Worldwide, Inc., the Tokyo Broadcasting System, the *Wall Street Journal,* the World Values Survey conducted by the World Values Study Group, the United States Information Agency, Yankelovich Partners, and the *Yomiuri Shimbun.* Professor Rolf Uher and his colleagues at the Zentralarchive fur Empirische Sozialforschung made the 1993 and 1994 Japanese surveys, conducted as part of the International Social Science Programme (ISSP), available to us on an expedited basis. Jim Marshall, senior research analyst and Japan survey expert at the United States Information Agency, read the manuscript and provided many helpful suggestions.

At the American Enterprise Institute, two interns, Ginger Crouch and Peter J. Baker, painstakingly entered data for the tables and proofread them over and over again. They and Melissa Knauer checked facts throughout. Melissa also read the manuscript to make all final corrections. AEI editor Cheryl Weissman read the manuscript carefully and offered many helpful suggestions. Jennifer Baggette, who worked at AEI for five years, began pulling together data on U.S.-Japanese attitudes early in her tenure at the institute. She also reviewed the manuscript—for which both authors want to express their thanks.

At the Roper Center, associate director John Barry and foreign data acquisitions manager David Wilber have played important roles in assembling the Japan survey data collection. Tatsuo Yamamoto has performed ably as research associate to the project and as chief translator. The work of two senior doctoral candidates specializing in Japanese politics—Misa Nishikawa and Gon Namkung—has been invaluable. Two other doctoral candidates specializing in American public opinion—Regina Dougherty and Cathy Flavin—helped assemble the data and reviewed the manuscript. Special thanks go to Rob Persons, who brought together much of the U.S. data presented in these pages.

Ladd is especially pleased to recognize the work of two close colleagues. Cathy Cuneo became his administrative assistant just as the preparation of this volume began in earnest. She helped prepare parts of the manuscript, and even more important, she ensured that many other projects stayed on course as work on the book proceeded. Lynn Zayachkiwsky, a colleague of fourteen years, participated in every facet of the book's preparation in her capacity as manager of Roper Center publications. The book would not have been completed either as quickly or as well without her active involvement.

E.C.L.
Storrs, Connecticut
K.H.B.
Washington, D.C.

CHAPTER 1

Two Nations Compared

August 1995 marked the fiftieth anniversary of the climactic events marking the end of World War II: the dropping of the first atomic bomb on Hiroshima on August 6, 1945; the dropping of the second bomb on Nagasaki on August 9; and the Japanese surrender on August 14. In the years since the war, Americans and Japanese, while in no sense forgetting the conflict or seeing it in the same light, have nonetheless put it largely behind them, establishing a vast and generally positive relationship. As the world's leading economic powers and as major trading partners, Americans and Japanese find their two countries inextricably linked.

Yet for all the importance of their ties, it is remarkably hard to find comparative data on the two countries—outside of basic economic statistics. Nowhere is the dearth of readily available information more evident than in the area touched by survey research. For more than sixty years, survey organizations in the United States have been exploring Americans' opinions, values, and self-assessments, and not incidentally asking how we see Japan. Polling developed in Japan only a little bit later. An article in the *Public Opinion Quarterly* (*POQ*) refers to a 1935 survey conducted by the Japanese Ministry of Education.[1] After the war and especially since 1970, polling expanded in both countries, yielding a mountain of data on how we see ourselves and each other. But for all the frequency and quality of this research, comparative data are hard to come by, even for those in government, business, the press, and academia, whose work makes United States-Japan comparisons highly relevant. Survey research is not the only means, of course, of seeing the two countries in comparative perspective; but

1. Andie Knutson, "Japanese Opinion Surveys: The Special Need and the Special Difficulties," *Public Opinion Quarterly*, vol. 9, no. 3 (1945), pp. 313–19.

1

it can provide information that is essential to understanding both similarities and differences in the outlook and values of these two nations' citizens, and in their perceptions of the ties between them. The purpose of this book is to review contemporary public opinion data on the United States and Japan, and to present the most important findings. Historical comparisons are brought in when they are relevant to present-day concerns.

Assembling an Archive

There is one very good reason why the comparative review presented here did not come earlier—even though the need for it seems evident in the two countries' close and important relationship. Although large numbers of polls are taken in both countries each year, no concerted effort had been made to assemble them in an accessible research library. This was a special problem in the case of Japan, where no archive brought together the total body of survey findings (although individual research organizations did maintain systematic collections of their own data).

This study has been made possible by the commitment of the Roper Center for Public Opinion Research at the University of Connecticut to collect and translate a large number of Japanese surveys. In 1992, the center received a grant from the Center for Global Partnership (CGP) of the Japan Foundation to start building an archive of Japanese survey data. The center has long been active in building and maintaining a U.S. opinion-data library and making it available to researchers, but it was unable to sustain the development of a Japan collection until the CGP gave its support. For the past three years, Roper Center staff have been acquiring new surveys from Japan, translating them, and entering the findings into an on-line information system. At present, the system is available for use in-house only, but the center looks forward to making it available electronically to researchers around the world—just as the center's U.S. data collection was made available through an on-line system, "POLL," in the mid 1980s. The Japan data bank at the Roper Center now contains approximately 32,000 survey questions and responses thereto, asked in Japan from 1979 to 1996. The center's library also houses about 130 Japanese survey datasets, going back to 1953.

Problems confronting United States-Japan comparisons do not end with the difficulties associated with gathering basic data. There are a host of other obstacles to any satisfactory comparative interpretation of the results. In the *POQ* article cited above, Andie Knutson identified some of these difficulties a half-century ago, while arguing strongly for an expanded use of the survey vehicle in building the peace between the two countries and enhancing commercial exchange.[2] He pointed out that the Japanese language had no equivalents for many common American expressions.

Knutson noted the abundance of homonyms in Japanese, making translation particularly treacherous. In the immediate postwar period, he tells us, Japanese society was still highly hierarchical, with different vocabularies and sentence structures for different groups, thus compounding the difficulties of taking national surveys. The social relationship between people in Japan dictates different levels of language and politeness, making it hard for pollsters to select the appropriate language for all people interviewed in a poll. He noted further that the Japanese have a habit of indirect expression not common in the United States. Our own review of thousands of questions revealed that Japanese are more likely than Americans to take middle positions in their responses to survey questions.

Given language barriers and cultural predispositions, scholars and others who use the data assembled here have to be especially careful in interpreting the results. Neither of the authors of this volume speaks Japanese. Neither is a student of Japanese politics and culture. We are confident that the Japan-United States data library described above will in the years ahead provide a resource that country specialists can utilize effectively. In the meantime, we believe that the broad comparisons we attempt here will make a contribution—both to mutual understanding of the views and values of Americans and Japanese, and as a stimulus to further research and analysis by teams of scholars who combine deep knowledge of both countries.

We have benefited greatly in preparing this book from the advice and counsel of a team of researchers assembled at the Roper Center as part of the Japan data bank project. Their contributions are noted in the preface. We have also drawn on the work of leading scholars of Japan and of comparative culture. Seymour Martin Lipset of the Hoover Institution and George Mason University, Kazufumi Manabe of Kwansei Gakuin University, and William Watts of Potomac Associates—to name only three—have written extensively about public attitudes in Japan. Their views have informed this study.

---

2. Ibid.

Overview of the Volume

Public Opinion in America and Japan is organized into five sections. We begin with a brief review of basic aggregate data on the two countries—information on characteristics of the two economies, information on patterns of consumption, and demographic variables (chapter 2). While our principal focus is on comparing opinions and values, economic and demographic information is an essential starting point in national comparisons. Work done by researchers at the Organization for Economic Cooperation and Development (OECD) is especially helpful in this regard.

Chapter 3 then reviews survey data in the area where the most extensive comparative work has been done—how Americans and Japanese view their countries' overarching relationship and their military, diplomatic, and economic ties and how these assessments have evolved over the past fifty years. Media companies in the United States and Japan have conducted many studies in these areas; available collections are much more complete for this than for any other substantive topic. Chapter 4 assesses survey findings on the two societies—the values that define us as peoples, the ideas that we hold about our families, work, religion, the relations between men and women, and the like. We also examine here levels of satisfaction and dissatisfaction in both countries with various aspects of daily life. Chapter 5 shifts to views of government, government's role in the economy, and assessments of governmental performance. In chapter 6 we conclude this review of comparative survey findings by focusing on the responses of young people in the two countries. Any systematic exploration of group differences lies beyond an overview like this one. We believe, however, that it is especially important—to the consideration of where these two societies are heading in the evolution of their thinking about social problems and in basic social values—to compare the views of their young people.

Tocqueville's Forecast of Global Democracy

No researcher should begin any exercise of comparison without some clear sense of the objects to which such comparison is properly pointing. Specifically here, apart from the obvious fact that the two countries are important and their futures intertwined, what is it that we want to know about them, their outlook, and their values? What questions or issues hold special importance or fascination? For the authors, the answer to these questions goes back to a grand hypothesis that Alexis de Tocqueville formed more than one hundred and fifty years ago. In this Frenchman's magisterial study of the young American nation, *Democracy in America,* Tocqueville argued that the whole planet would eventually be engulfed in a titanic social revolution, in which the United States was the pioneer or pathbreaker. The collapse of traditional ascriptive-class or aristocratic societies and their replacement by more egalitarian, individualist, and democratic systems was a transition that Tocqueville believed inevitable—even though he predicted it would occur at different rates of speed, would manifest itself with different social costs, and would be shaped by various national traditions. "I confess," he said, "that in America I saw more than America; I sought there an image of democracy itself with its inclinations, its character, its prejudices, and its passions, in order to learn what we have to fear or to hope from its progress."[3]

The American experience was to be studied, then, for what it told about aspects of everyone's future—though Tocqueville believed the way America entered the modern world was entirely exceptional. "There is one country in the world in which this great social revolution seems almost to have reached its natural limits; it took place in a simple, easy fashion, or rather one might say that that country sees the results of the democratic revolution taking place among us, without experiencing the revolution itself," Tocqueville argued. "The emigrants who colonized America at the beginning of the seventeenth century in some way separated the principle of democracy from all those other principles against which they contended when living in the heart of the old European societies, and transplanted that principle only on the shores of the New World."[4]

Many later analysts have seen Tocqueville's interpretation as an essential starting point for understanding American social, economic, and political development. Louis Hartz built his account of American exceptionalism entirely upon it.[5] Seymour Martin Lipset has, similarly, drawn on Tocqueville's great insight in much of his writing, including *The First New Nation* and *American Exceptionalism.*[6]

---

3. Alexis de Tocqueville, *Democracy in America* (New York: Anchor Books, 1969), p. 19.
4. Ibid, pp. 18–19.
5. Louis Hartz, *The Liberal Tradition in America* (New York: Harcourt, Brace & World, 1955).
6. Seymour Martin Lipset, *The First New Nation* (New York: W.W. Norton and Co., 1967); and Lipset, *American Exceptionalism: A Double-edged Sword* (New York: W.W. Norton, 1996).

As Lipset has observed,

> Efforts to account for America's past success . . . have emphasized that as compared to Europe, it had fewer encrusted pre-industrial traditions to overcome. . . . [I]n particular, that it had never been a feudal or hierarchical state church–dominated society. All of Europe and '. . . Japan was once feudal, organized in terms of monarchy, aristocracy and fixed hierarchy, with a value system embedded in institutions that both emphasized the virtues inherent in agrarian society and deprecated commercial activities.[7]

But while Tocqueville emphasized the unique way in which America experienced modernity, he at the same time argued that all nations would in their own ways encounter it. He wrote in his introduction to *Democracy* that "it seems to me beyond doubt that sooner or later we, like the Americans, will attain almost complete equality of conditions." He quickly added that "I certainly do not draw from that the conclusion that we are necessarily destined one day to derive the same political consequences as the Americans from the similar social state." He was, he went on, "very far from believing that they have found the only form possible for democratic government. . . ." Still, if each nation would have to move from the old order to the new through its own course, each would in fact experience it, like it or not.

> I have not even claimed to judge whether the progress of the social revolution, which I consider irresistible, is profitable or prejudicial for mankind. I accept that revolution as an accomplished fact, or a fact that soon will be accomplished, and I selected of all the peoples experiencing it that nation in which it has come to the fullest and most peaceful completion, in order to see its natural consequences clearly, and if possible, to turn it to the profit of mankind.

Was Tocqueville right? Not in the short run, the history of the past century and a half has shown us; but then, Tocqueville's perspective was anything but short-term. In the long run, he argued, principles of egalitarianism, individualism, and democracy would sweep the planet—not necessarily without great pain.

Comparison of America and Japan represents, then, an opportunity to pursue Tocqueville's grand hypothesis. The two countries

---

7. Lipset, *American Exceptionalism*, p. 211.

remain very different in certain social values. America, so stridently individualist when Tocqueville visited it in the 1830s, is the same today. But if Japan today strikes Americans as collectivistic and traditional, there seems to us little doubt—as the survey data here attest—that, having achieved advanced industrial status, that country is moving, on its own terms, toward an ever more insistent assertion of egalitarianism and individuality. The American-Japanese comparison seems to support the idea of convergence in broad societal-value terms—though it naturally rejects simplistic ideas of Japan's becoming "Americanized," or of the two nations somehow becoming "the same." The phenomenon is a more elaborate and interesting one—of two countries being propelled along a course, at varying speeds, from differing histories, to which the very idea of modernity points.

CHAPTER 2

Economy and Demography

For two decades now, discussions of America and Japan have often begun and ended with their respective economies. And much of the discussion has been alarmist. Harvard sociologist Ezra Vogel was not the first to write about Japan in this way, but his *Japan as Number 1: Lessons for the United States* (1979) gave economic alarmism extraordinary currency in both countries. A drumbeat of accounts in the 1980s contrasted manufacturing prowess in Japan with increasing impotence in the United States. Stories of purchases of prime U.S. real estate by Japanese business interests—such as Mitsubishi's purchase of New York's Rockefeller complex in 1989—were widely cited as the visible symbols of a deep-seated change in the two countries' relative economic positions—a change that would purportedly leave Americans struggling to live in a declining economy. The U.S. balance-of-payments deficit in trade with Japan was also often cited as proof of U.S. economic weakness.

"Red Sun rising" hyperbole has diminished, to be sure, in recent years. The Tokyo stock exchange crashed in 1989. The Japanese economy entered a recession that saw average annual growth rates of less than 1 percent for three years. In 1995, the financial weakness of Japanese banks added further to already growing doubts about Japanese economic dominance. In October 1995, for example, the U.S. Federal Reserve arranged to provide Japanese financial institutions, in the case of a sudden liquidity crisis, with billions of dollars—literally overnight—in exchange for Japanese Treasury bonds and bills. In the wake of such developments, a new alarmist literature citing Japanese economic weakness has appeared.[1]

---

1. See, for example, Brian Reading, *Japan: The Coming Collapse* (London: Weidenfeld & Nicholson, 1992); and Christopher Wood, *The Bubble Economy: The Japanese Economic Collapse* (New York: Atlantic Monthly Press, 1992).

Perhaps it is only an irresistible urge to sell books, but authors seem unable to describe the U.S. and Japanese economies in terms other than apocalyptic. Recently, amid the stream of bad economic news from Japan, Eamon Fingleton published a book arguing that "Japan is still on track to overtake the United States by the year 2000."[2] He sees "the stage . . . set for Japan to surpass the United States to become the world's largest economy. . . . It is a prospect Americans are singularly unprepared for." It seems to us that this rush for the bold and apocalyptic creates a badly distorted picture of the considerable accomplishments of both economies, whose comparative standings have evolved rather predictably, each maintaining areas of strength and relative weakness.

Economic Strengths

Currency exchange rates are inadequate as instruments for calculating the relative sizes and patterns of growth of national economies. Measuring according to exchange rates causes the U.S. economy to appear larger than it actually is during periods when the dollar is overpriced, and smaller than it is when the yen is strong. Foolishness and absurdity have been perpetrated by researchers who have taken dollar income for families in the United States and yen income for Japanese families, gone to the exchange rate tables in the daily newspaper, multiplied, and presented the comparative figures as reliable descriptions of the national income stories.

Recognizing that exchange rates tell very little about the price people pay for the goods and services they must buy in their domestic economies, economists at the Organisation for Economic Co-operation and Development (OECD) introduced in the early 1980s a vastly more satisfactory tool, which they have called *purchasing power parities* (PPPs). These are international price indexes linking the price levels of different countries. The methodology used by the OECD involves valuing the goods and services sold in different countries according to a common set of international prices. PPPs show how many units of currency are needed in one country to buy the same amount of goods and services that one unit of currency will buy in the other country. For example, how many French francs are needed to buy in France what one U.S. dollar will buy in the United States?

2. Eamon Fingleton, *Blindside: Why Japan Is Still on Track to Overtake the United States by the Year 2000* (New York: Houghton Mifflin Co., 1995).

Working with its PPP calculations, OECD researchers have charted the progression of member countries' economies for more than a quarter century now. Table A–1 shows the United States, Japan, and the entire OECD average. (The economic and demographic tables are printed in the appendix. Tables dealing with attitudinal data appear in the text.) By the early 1980s, Japan had reached essential parity with the average for all OECD countries, and in the mid-1990s it surpassed the average by a substantial margin. Yet while the Japanese economy has made impressive relative gains, it remains well behind the United States in per capita gross domestic product (GDP), as measured by the PPP equivalents.

This volume, devoted primarily to reviewing survey research findings on the two countries' opinions and values, is obviously not the place for any detailed examination of strengths and weaknesses or other characteristics of the two economies. That undertaking is far too complex. But the economic data are especially relevant because even in broad-brush comparison, they powerfully contradict the alarmist descriptions that have predominated in the United States and that appear common in Japan as well. The basic trade statistics are well known, and they show the United States running a continuing balance-of-trade (current accounts) deficit, while Japan has maintained a substantial surplus (table A–2).

In many other areas, however, the data show developments quite at odds with the picture generally disseminated, in the U.S. media at least. For example, Japanese manufacturing has an impressive record. Nonetheless, OECD data show that U.S. manufacturing in general has held its own. In the 1990s, with Japan's economy in recession, U.S. manufacturing output has grown modestly, while Japan's output has declined. In the latter half of the 1980s, by contrast, Japan's manufacturing production climbed more rapidly than that of the United States, but only slightly so. The same was true for the first half of the 1980s (table A–3).

Despite all the talk about America's "eating its seed corn" in terms of a low saving rate (compared with a much higher saving rate in Japan), both countries invest at high levels in their economic futures. For example, table A–4 shows each country making comparable per capita expenditures for research and development. The OECD average for R & D—again, per capita, in PPP equivalents—was only $286 (half the level it was in both the United States and Japan) in 1993, the latest year for which data are available. When it comes to the high-technology balance of payments, OECD data show the United

10

States selling a lot of high-tech products, buying relatively few, and enjoying a balance far larger and more positive than that for any other OECD country.

Education is another area where current spending, assuming it is well applied, represents an investment in the nation's economic future, just as in the first instance it is an investment in each individual receiving it. The United States is a great net importer of talented students into its higher education system, Japan a net exporter (especially to the United States). The United States far surpasses Japan in total spending for education at all levels—primary and secondary as well as university, according to OECD data. Japan is essentially a middle-of-the-pack country in educational expenditures, compared with the OECD world at large (table A–5). Analysts credit Japanese primary and secondary schools with being very good "at turning out uniformly qualified high school graduates. . . . Japanese education tends to be serious (for instance, twice as much classroom time is spent learning math at the elementary level), and students and teachers alike work harder (the Japanese school year is 240 days, versus 180 in the United States, and each day is longer)."[3] A higher proportion of Japanese high-school graduates continue on to advanced training than do graduates in most other countries, but rates of matriculation to college in Japan remain below those in the United States (table A–5).

In chapter 3, we discuss perceptions of the U.S.-Japanese economic relationship. These data focus on current attitudes and do not give much sense of the dramatic change in U.S. perceptions of Japan that has accompanied Japan's economic advance. In 1971, for example, when Louis Harris and Associates began its work for the *Asahi Shimbun,* Americans were divided over whether Japanese goods were of high quality (35 percent said they were) or cheaply made or undependable (33 percent gave this response). Forty-six percent in a separate question in the survey agreed with the view that the Japanese were "very good at copying and imitating other people's products and inventions, but not much good at developing their own" (36 percent disagreed). Of those who had purchased a Japanese-made product (58 percent of those surveyed), most said it was either a toy, a radio, or a camera. The ambivalent view of Japanese products did not suggest that Americans thought the Japanese were lazy. In the

---

3. Karl Zinsmeister, "Shadows on the Rising Sun," *The American Enterprise,* May–June 1990, p. 54.

poll, Americans said they liked and admired the Japanese work ethic more than any other of a long list of personal qualities. American admiration of Japanese work habits has been a constant finding in survey data since the war.

In its work for the *Asahi Shimbun*, Louis Harris surveyed Americans again in 1982 and found that popular impressions of Japanese products had shifted significantly. The number of Americans rating Japanese goods as being of high quality had nearly doubled, from 35 percent to 69 percent. In 1982, only 19 percent felt that Japanese goods were cheaply made or undependable, a sharp drop from a decade before. In both surveys, young people (we review their attitudes in chapter 6) were more likely than older people to say Japanese goods were of high quality. Far fewer nationally in 1982 than in 1971 (31 compared with 46 percent) said the Japanese were good only at copying others' products. Once again, Japanese diligence and hard work were admired more than any other of a long list of personal qualities. The frictions in our current economic relationship must be seen in the context of the significant regard Americans have for the qualities that have contributed to Japan's economic rise.

Daily Life

When it comes to consumption habits, Americans and Japanese present interesting similarities and contrasts. Households in both countries are loaded with the basic "consumer durables"—color TVs and microwaves (table A–6). At the same time, in other key areas, the average Japanese consumes much less than his or her American counterpart. He or she lives in a considerably smaller dwelling, for example—2,000 square feet on average in America, compared with fewer than 1,000 square feet per average residence in Japan. Interestingly, some aspects of "consumer infrastructure" are much less developed in Japan than in other advanced industrial nations. For example, fewer than half of Japanese homes have sewer hookups.

In other areas, though, many observers would see the lower rates of Japanese consumption as a positive indicator. For example, the average Japanese takes in nearly 1,000 fewer calories a day than his or her American counterpart, and consumes only half as much in fats. This may contribute in part to Japanese men and women's experiencing longer life expectancy (table A–6). Per capita consumption of energy (electricity and other forms) is also far lower in Japan than in America. Americans have more television receivers, but the Japanese read far more newspapers. U.S. newspaper readership continues to lag well behind the levels in most other industrial democracies.

The family unit is more cohesive in Japan than in the United States, and many households include grandparents. There are almost twice as many extended family units in Japan as there are in the United States (18 compared with 10 percent). The percentage of married-couple households has not changed in Japan over the past thirty years, while it has dropped significantly in the United States. Eight percent of American households, compared with just 2 percent of those in Japan, are single-parent households (table A–6). In the child-centered culture of Japan, most children grow up in married-couple families—one explanation for the relatively low child poverty rate there. In the United States, in 1993, 71 percent of children lived in two-parent households, a drop from 85 percent in 1970. If present trends continue, a significant proportion (roughly 60 percent) of children born in the United States will spend at least some time in a single-parent household. In Japan in 1990, 1 percent of births were to unmarried women. In the United States, 30 percent were, up from 11 percent in 1970. The divorce rate in the United States is now roughly twice what it was in 1960, though it leveled off over the past decade. The divorce rate in Japan, in contrast, has been both low and relatively stable.

It should be noted, however, that the survey research–derived picture of divorce in Japan significantly understates reality. A January 1994 NHK survey found, for example, only 4 percent of adult Japanese indicating that they had ever been divorced—compared with findings in the range of 25 to 30 percent of adult Americans (table A–7). When official government statistics on divorces are examined, however, one sees that the actual incidence of divorce in Japan, while much lower than in the United States, is not nearly so much lower as the poll findings suggest (table A–8). Fewer Japanese who have been divorced are willing to acknowledge it to a stranger in an opinion survey than is true of their counterparts in the United States.

The number of large families has declined greatly in every advanced industrial democracy. But although they are the exception, large (three children and more) families remain more common in the United States than in other industrial nations. Asked in a survey done for the World Values Study Group in the early 1990s whether they had had any children, 33 percent of Americans said they had had three or more, compared with just 20 percent of Japanese (table A–9). Government birth statistics show that since 1957, fertility rates in Japan have remained essentially constant at about 1.8 births per woman, a bit below the population replacement level. Similarly, low levels obtain in many industrial democracies, but the Japanese experience in the decade or so after World War II was very different from that in these other countries. There was a small rise in the birth rate in Japan just after the war, but from 1947 to 1957 fertility rates fell sharply from 4.5 lifetime births per woman to just 2.0. During that time, other industrial nations were in the midst of a baby boom.

Yet if actual birth rates have been low in Japan for the past half-century, child-centered Japan still considers larger families to be the ideal. Asked in the World Values Survey conducted by the World Values Study Group (1990–1993) what they thought was the ideal family size, 55 percent of adult Japanese said three or more children (48 percent of this 55 percent total said three children), compared with just 41 percent of Americans favoring a three-children-or-larger family as the ideal. Thus, the average American family is larger than the average Japanese family, and has been larger for the entire post–World War span—but more Japanese than Americans posit a large family as the "desired" norm (table A–8). Younger people in Japan and the United States, as we will see later, tend to prefer two-children families.[4]

Demographic expert Karl Zinsmeister has observed that "the population of Japan is aging faster than any on earth. In one lifetime, from 1947 to 2025, Japan will go from being one of the globe's youngest nations (with less than 5 percent of its population 65 years old or more) to quite likely the oldest (with nearly one-fourth of all citizens elderly)."[5] A cabinet-level agency responsible for long-term planning calls elder care Japan's biggest looming crisis. Zinsmeister goes on to note that, looked at in terms of changes occurring in the median age of the population, "Japan is now aging twice as fast as the United States." The recent past in this transformation is shown in tables A–10 and A–11. Both the United States and Japan now have larger proportions of their population in the sixty-five-years-and older range than they had in 1970, but the upward shift is modest in the United States (from 10 percent in 1970 to 13 percent in 1993), compared with Japan (rising from 7 percent in 1970 to 14 percent in 1993).

Despite its rapidly aging population, Japan has managed to moderate increases in health-care spending. Between 1983 and 1993,

---

4. For example, the Dentsu/Virginia Slims data show eighteen–through–twenty-nine-year-olds in Japan preferring two-children families.

5. Karl Zinsmeister, "Raising Hiroko," *The American Enterprise*, March-April 1990, p. 55.

OECD data show, the proportion of GDP expended for health care in Japan remained constant, while that in the United States increased substantially. In 1993 the United States was spending roughly twice as much of its GDP (14 percent compared with 7 percent) on health costs as was Japan (table A–12). No other industrial democracy was spending as much on health as was America.

The United States and Japan are both relatively low-tax countries, compared with the rest of the OECD world (table A–13). In terms of public spending, the two countries look most dramatically different in the area of national defense. We explore Japanese thinking about their armed forces and defense efforts in chapter 3. The experience of World War II, the country's defeat and devastation, and the subsequent U.S. occupation of the country have naturally produced an aversion to military expenditures and commitments that is dramatically different from what the United States, as the victor, has experienced. Table A–14 shows just how much less as a proportion of the GDP Japan is now spending for national defense. The American military presence in Japan remains a substantial one—with more than 16,000 U.S. military personnel stationed in mainland Japan and 24,000 in Okinawa. This presence has been a source of continuing tensions—as the reaction to the kidnapping and rape of a schoolgirl by U.S. military personnel in Okinawa in September 1995 attests.

The economic and demographic data above provide a portrait of two advanced industrial nations. Survey data add to the picture in important respects by fleshing out other connections between the two societies. In 1971, in the Louis Harris survey for the *Asahi Shimbun*, 8 percent of Americans said they had visited Japan. Of this small group, 60 percent had been part of the American occupation forces, another 10 percent had been coming or going from Vietnam, and 7 percent had been there in connection with the Korean War. Seven in ten of the American visitors said they enjoyed their stay, and more than eight in ten wanted to return. Of the population as a whole, two-thirds wanted to visit Japan. At that time, 31 percent of the Americans surveyed said they personally knew someone who was Japanese (the percentage was 62 percent in the western United States). In a March 1995 survey done by the Hart/Teeter Research Companies for the *Wall Street Journal* and the *Nihon Keizai Shimbun*, 10 percent of Americans said they had visited Japan, as compared with slightly more than a quarter (26 percent) of the Japanese who had visited the United States. Forty percent of Americans knew someone who was a Japanese citizen, while 58 percent did not. Twenty-six percent of the Japanese knew an American citizen.

In a 1992 Yankelovich Partners survey conducted in the United States for *Time* and CNN and in Japan by Infoplan/Yankelovich International, a near majority in the United States (47 percent) said they felt they knew a lot or some things about Japan. Fifty-five percent of the Japanese surveyed gave those responses about the United States. Far more Japanese had studied American history in school (62 percent) than Americans had studied Japanese history (32 percent). Five percent of the Japanese said they spoke English fairly fluently, and 37 percent said they spoke it somewhat. Only 5 percent of Americans gave either of those responses to a question about speaking Japanese. In a 1989 CBS News/*New York Times*/Toyko Broadcasting System survey, one-quarter in the United States and 10 percent in Japan said they could carry on a simple conversation in a language other than their own.

Surveys also confirm the spread of a global popular culture. In the *Wall Street Journal/Nihon Keizai Shimbun* March 1995 survey, 80 percent of the Japanese had a very or fairly positive view of American popular culture. (In this survey, the Germans—the only other nation surveyed—were more dubious.) In the 1986 Louis Harris/*Asahi Shimbun* survey, Americans could identify Yoko Ono far more than any other Japanese artist or politician or businessman.

Yet another manifestation of our cultural interaction comes from awareness of each other's food. In the 1971 Louis Harris survey, more Americans disliked than liked Japanese food (42 versus 27 percent), but a significant three in ten were not sure. By 1982 in the same collaboration, a majority of Americans told the surveyors that they liked Japanese food. By 1986, Japanese food was becoming so well known in the United States that Americans were asked about specific kinds. Forty-four percent had tasted sukiyaki, 34 percent sushi, 28 percent tempura. (In mid-1995, Roper Starch Worldwide, Inc. reported that sushi's popularity in the United States was on the wane, as it had never transcended the young, upscale-professional market to catch on with other groups in the population.) American food is very popular in Japan, too, as the proliferation of fast-food outlets attests. That familiar American icon, Coca-Cola, was introduced in Japan in 1919. Baseball is also a common interest in both places. In 1982 Harris found that 90 percent of Americans knew that Japan had professional baseball.

From World War II to the present, both Americans and Japanese have had reasons aplenty—though different reasons—for mutual antipathy. In fact, however, because of the economic and social interactions and the development of a global popular culture, the story of the two people's postwar relations is more one of comity than of conflict. We explore this extraordinary dimension of the American-Japanese relationship in chapter 3.

CHAPTER 3

The Military and Economic Relationship

Six years before Pearl Harbor, pollster Elmo Roper posed the first question that we have discovered concerning Americans' views of Japan. He included it as part of his then continuing survey work for *Fortune* magazine. Respondents were asked toward which foreign countries they felt "least" and "most" friendly. Not surprisingly given the historic ties, we felt most friendly toward England (cited by 29 percent). Of the seven other countries Roper tested, China and Japan ranked last in approval. Half of those surveyed answered "all," "none," or "don't know" to both questions. Roper's commentary about this finding has a surprisingly contemporary ring. He notes Americans' "blithe indifference to foreign affairs," a criticism of Americans that has been heard in foreign policy circles ever since.[1]

In his coverage for *Fortune*, Roper continued:

> But when events threaten to invade our sense of security, there is danger of a strong emotional reaction having little to do with the political realism we apply to our own affairs. With the peace of Munich, for example, something seemed to snap in the American mind. Out of indifference toward all foreign people came an upsurge of anti-German sentiment; from isolation came a swing toward the idea of collective security in a democratic front against aggression.[2]

Americans are slow to anger, but once provoked they are determined in whatever course they choose. By November of 1940, on Japan's formal announcement that she had joined the Axis, Roper found that a near majority, 49 percent of those surveyed, felt that the

---

1. Elmo Roper, "The *Fortune* Survey," *Fortune*, October 1935, p. 170.
2. Ibid., October 1939, p. 82.

time had come for the United States to take stronger measures against Japan. Only a quarter dissented, and slightly more had not made up their minds.

By early 1941, U.S. opinion had hardened markedly with regard to both fronts in the war. As for Europe, Americans no longer thought there could be any easy way out. Two-thirds of those interviewed by Gallup in a survey of March 9–14 said U.S. policy should be "to help England win even at the risk of getting into the war [ourselves]," rather than "to keep out of the war [ourselves]." The isolationist approach was backed by just one in three. Although polling on Japan and the war in Asia was less extensive, it clearly reflected a similar hardening of attitudes. Between August 21 and 26, 1941, Gallup asked whether it should be U.S. policy to "take steps now to keep Japan from becoming more powerful, even if it means risking a war with Japan." Seventy percent endorsed this policy, while only 18 percent opposed it, and 12 percent had no opinion. Support was even more decisive in the western United States. In a survey taken November 27–December 1, just a week or so before the attack on Pearl Harbor, 52 percent polled by Gallup said they thought "the United States will go to war against Japan some time in the near future"; only 27 percent disagreed.

The War and Its Legacy

If Americans are slow to anger yet decisive once engaged, they are also quick to forgive. In August 1951, only five years after 63 percent of Americans told Gallup they believed the Japanese "entirely approved" of the killing and starving of prisoners, 51 percent said their attitudes toward the Japanese people were friendly, and only a quarter described them as unfriendly.

Contemporary survey data today confirm that for residents of both countries, the war appears to be all in the past. Eighty-six percent of Americans gave that response to a July 1995 CBS News/Toyko Broadcasting System poll.[3] Japanese responses were similar. Seventy-four percent said the war was all in the past (table 3–1). Not surprisingly, in both countries, those over sixty-five years of age were less likely than younger respondents to take this view.

---

3. The CBS News/Tokyo Broadcasting System collaboration has produced twelve surveys in each country since 1985. Most of the polls have been taken by CBS News/*New York Times*/Tokyo Broadcasting System. The May 1988, June–July 1989, and June–July 1995 surveys are CBS News and Toyko Broadcasting System only.

TABLE 3–1
PRESENCE OF HOSTILITY IN AMERICANS AND JAPANESE AS A RESULT OF
WORLD WAR II, 1971–1995
(percent)

Question: Do you personally still feel any hostility toward, or fear of,
Japan or the Japanese as a result of World War II, or not?

	Feel Hostility or Fear	Do Not
Americans		
1971	20	75
1982	14	84

Question: These days, do you sometimes think of the (Japanese/
Americans) as enemies because of World War II, or is that all in the
past?

	Enemies	All in the Past
Americans		
July 1985	11	85
Feb. 1989	11	84
Nov. 1991	14	83
July 1995	11	86
Japanese		
Feb. 1989	17	83
July 1995	23	74

NOTE: Not all response categories are shown.
SOURCES: For top panel, surveys by Louis Harris and Associates for *Asahi
Shimbun*, latest that of March 1982. For bottom panel, surveys by CBS
News/*New York Times* (U.S.) and the Tokyo Broadcasting System (Japan), lat-
est that of July 1995.

The first survey in the CBS News/*New York Times*/Tokyo Broadcasting System (hereafter referred to as CBS/NYT/TBS) collaboration in 1985 provides another indication that the war has receded in
our memories. Only 12 percent of Americans in the July 1985 survey
spontaneously said that they think of the war when asked what comes
to their minds when they hear the word "Japan." Just 7 percent of
Japanese mentioned the war. In the February 1989 CBS/NYT/TBS
poll, only 24 percent of Americans felt George Bush should not

attend Emperor Hirohito's funeral, because of memories of the war. (Again, a respondent's age affected the response. Those over age sixty-five were evenly split, with 41 percent saying that he should attend and 41 percent that he should not. Younger respondents by large majorities wanted the U.S. president to go.)

In terms of the war's most painful memories—Pearl Harbor, Hiroshima, and Nagasaki—polls again demonstrate that old wounds are healing. The CBS/NYT/TBS collaboration has asked the Japanese on four separate occasions whether they resent the United States for dropping atomic bombs on Hiroshima and Nagasaki. In December 1994 and July 1995, a majority said they did not resent the United States for the action (table 3–2), though a solid majority (70 percent in July 1995) in a separate question felt that their countrymen generally did. A majority of Japanese also felt that most Americans still resent their country for attacking Pearl Harbor. In fact, a majority or near majority of Americans in five separate askings said they did not resent the Japanese for attacking Pearl Harbor (table 3–2). Once again, more Americans felt that their fellow citizens still held Pearl Harbor against the Japanese than felt that way themselves. And again, majorities of Americans thought most Japanese resented the United States for bombing Hiroshima and Nagasaki.

Both Americans and Japanese describe Japan as the aggressor in the war, and majorities of those surveyed in the United States continue to approve of the decision to use the atomic bomb on Hiroshima and Nagasaki. Gallup first asked this question in 1945, when 85 percent approved. In 1990 when Gallup picked up the question again, 53 percent approved. In three separate askings since that time, a majority has continued to approve. Louis Harris and Associates surveys for the *Asahi Shimbun* in 1971, 1982, and 1986 support the Gallup results (table 3–3). The CBS/NYT/TBS collaboration explores the issue differently, asking whether dropping the atomic bombs on Japan in World War II was morally wrong. In July 1995, 34 percent of those surveyed in the United States agreed, while 58 percent disagreed. In Japan, 89 percent thought the action was morally wrong, and 11 percent disagreed. A question posed in Japan by the *Asahi Shimbun* in December 1994 was phrased differently and produced these responses: 44 percent told the interviewers that the U.S. nuclear attacks constituted unacceptable, inhumane behavior; 17 percent said the actions were inhumane but that the respondent no longer resented it; 22 percent said that the United States had to do what it did; and 15 percent said it was the proper thing to do because it was wartime.

TABLE 3–2

U.S. AND JAPANESE ATTITUDES TOWARD PEARL HARBOR, HIROSHIMA, AND
NAGASAKI, 1985–1995
(percent)

Question: Today, do you hold it against Japan for attacking Pearl
Harbor, or don't you hold it against them, or don't you know enough
about that to have an opinion?

	Hold It Against	Don't Hold
Americans		
July 1985	27	50
Feb. 1989	34	46
Nov. 1991	27	47
Dec. 1994	36	43
July 1995	29	46

Question: These days, do you hold it against the United States for dropping atomic bombs on Hiroshima and Nagasaki, or do you not hold it
against them, or don't you know enough about it to have an opinion?

Japanese		
July 1985	44	47
Nov. 1991	50	43
Dec. 1994	34	57
July 1995	43	55

NOTE: Not all response categories are shown.
SOURCE: Surveys by CBS News/*New York Times* (U.S.) and the Tokyo Broadcasting System (Japan), latest that of July 1995.

U.S. respondents in a March 1995 *Wall Street Journal/Nihon Keizai
Shimbun* poll (hereafter referred to as WSJ/NKS) felt that dropping
the atomic bombs was necessary to bring the war to an end (by a
majority of 68 percent affirmative responses to 25 percent dissent-
ing); Japanese respondents disagreed by roughly the same margin
(67 to 27 percent). One suggested argument that is rejected deci-
sively by the publics in both countries is that the United States used
the atomic bomb on the Japanese because they are not white. In a
December 1994 CBS/NYT/TBS survey, 64 percent of the Japanese
and 85 percent of the Americans disagreed with the idea that "one

TABLE 3–3
AMERICAN APPROVAL OF DROPPING THE ATOMIC BOMB, 1945–1995
(percent)

Question: Do you approve or disapprove of using the new atomic bomb on Japanese cities? (1945) As you may know, the United States dropped atomic bombs on Hiroshima and Nagasaki in August 1945, near the end of World War II. Looking back, would you say you approve or disapprove of using the atomic bomb on Japanese cities in 1945?

	Approve	*Disapprove*
1945	85	10
1990	53	41
1991	53	41
1994	55	39
1995	59	35

Question: Do you feel it was necessary and proper for the United States to drop atomic bombs on Japan during World War II, or do you think we were wrong to drop the bombs?

	Necessary and Proper	*We Were Wrong*
1971	64	21
1982	63	26
1986	67	24

NOTES: Not all response categories are shown.
An August 1995 Louis Harris and Associates survey for TV-Asahi found that 66 percent of Americans thought "the U.S. was justified in dropping the atomic bombs on Japan during World War II." Twenty-six percent said the United States was not justified.
SOURCES: For top panel, surveys by the Gallup Organization, latest that of July 1995. For bottom panel, surveys by Louis Harris and Associates for the *Asahi Shimbun*, latest that of October 1986.

of the major reasons that the United States was willing to drop the atomic bombs on Japan was because the Japanese people are not white." The question was also asked in 1985 and 1991; in each poll, majorities in both countries disagreed with the statement.

The issue of whether and what kind of a formal apology should be made was debated widely in Japan as the fiftieth anniversary of the war's end approached. In the CBS/NYT/TBS poll, majorities in

Japan in 1991 (55 percent) and 1995 (62 percent) thought their country should apologize to the United States for Pearl Harbor, whereas Americans were split. In July 1995, 46 percent of Americans said an apology should be given, 46 percent said it should not. In both years, more Japanese than Americans thought an apology should be given to America.

In the July 1995 CBS/NYT/TBS poll, just 17 percent of Americans said the U.S. government should formally apologize for Hiroshima and Nagasaki, and 76 percent said we should not. The Japanese were emphatic that we should (68 to 31 percent). The results did not differ significantly from those obtained in 1991. In a March 1995 question posed by WSJ/NKS, 38 percent of those in the United States said that Japan had done enough to take responsibility for its role in World War II; 53 percent said it had not. (Forty-five percent of Americans felt Germany had done enough.) The Japanese concurred about their own contrition, but by a more decisive margin. Sixty-one percent of the Japanese said Japan had not done enough to take responsibility, 29 percent that it had.

Military and Diplomatic Relations Today

Questions asked about the war in both countries provide impressive evidence that the event has receded in public memory and that the hostility of war has been replaced by substantial concord. A series of questions asked in both countries underscores the rapprochement. Still, differences in perspective—a legacy of the war—produce tensions. These, as well as the underlying strengths that Japanese and Americans see in their relationship, are the topics we will explore next.

In Japan, wariness of the use of military force or of military involvement is widespread and long-standing, and these sentiments inform many contemporary poll questions. Article 9 of the American-sponsored Japanese Constitution contains the passage: "Aspiring sincerely to an international peace based on justice and order, the Japanese people forever renounce war as a sovereign right of the nation and the threat or use of force as a means of settling international disputes." The passage continues that "land, sea, and air forces, as well as other war potential, will never be maintained."[4] But three years later, when South Korea was invaded, General Douglas MacArthur, supreme com-

---

4. John K. Emmerson and Leonard A. Humphreys, *Will Japan Rearm?* (AEI-Hoover Policy Studies, 1973), p. 116.

mander of the Allied Forces of the Pacific, ordered the Japanese to form a 75,000-man "police reserve force," arguing that in the climate of international lawlessness "it is inherent that this ideal [the renunciation of war] must give way to the overwhelming law of self-preservation and it will become your duty . . . in concert with others who cherish freedom to mount force to repel force."[5] The Allied Treaty of Peace with Japan of September 1951 states that as a sovereign nation, Japan "possesses the inherent right of individual or collective self-defense" specified in the United Nations Charter and that she may voluntarily "enter into collective security arrangements."[6] The treaty also states that American occupation forces will be removed and that Japan may enter into bilateral or multilateral agreements with one or more of the Allied powers. Until recently, the Socialists have challenged the constitutionality of Japan's Self-Defense Forces, and the principle of renunciation of war is deeply embedded in Japanese consciousness.

In yearly surveys conducted for the Prime Minister's Office since 1987, three-quarters or more of the Japanese have agreed with the statement: "Japan is consistently pacifistic." In 1994, for example, 83 percent of the Japanese concurred. In June 1991, *Asahi Shimbun* surveyors asked whether Japan should strictly respect the principle of renunciation of war in its Constitution. A majority (56 percent) wanted a strict interpretation of Article 9, and about a third said it could be flexibly construed. Japan does not see itself as a military power, nor does it expect to become one. The CBS/NYT/TBS polling group asked the Japanese five times between 1985 and 1991 whether they thought of Japan as a strong or weak military power. The highest "strong" response was 35 percent in November 1991. A January 1995 *Yomiuri Shimbun* survey that asked the Japanese whether they expected Japan to be a military power produced these responses: 19 percent said yes, 74 percent no, with only 3 percent offering the view that Japan was a military power now.

Not only do the Japanese reject the use of force as a guiding principle for themselves, but they also believe in extending the principle beyond their borders. Only 26 percent of Japanese in the November 1991 CBS/NYT/TBS poll felt that it is appropriate to use military force "to maintain international justice and order"; 70 percent said this is not appropriate. Americans' responses reflected a mirror image: 72 percent said using force is appropriate, 26 percent said that it is not.

---

5. Ibid., pp. 7–8.
6. Ibid., p. 117.

In the same poll, a majority of Americans (63 percent) agreed that the United States has a responsibility to "take military action in trouble spots around the world when it is asked by its allies"; a majority of Japanese (52 percent) disagreed that this is a U.S. responsibility. During the Vietnam and Persian Gulf wars, Japanese opposition to military involvement produced tensions in our relationship.

Underscoring the Japanese disposition toward pacifism are the results of survey questions asked recently about permanent Japanese membership on the United Nations Security Council. The Japanese (like the Americans) approve of the general idea of Japan's membership. In an October 1994 survey for the Prime Minister's Office, of the 56 percent approving, a majority said they approved because "the addition of Japan, which does not possess nuclear weapons and advocates pacifism, would contribute to peace." Of the 18 percent disapproving of the idea, the primary reason was concern that membership would require Japanese involvement in UN military activities. A question asked by *Asahi Shimbun* surveyors in September 1994 found 57 percent disagreeing with Japan's membership if Japan "would be required to play a military role." Twenty-nine percent said Japan should become a member under these circumstances.

For Americans, awareness of the global leadership role that became America's after World War II informs national responses to questions about international involvement today. In 29 separate askings of a question first posed by the National Opinion Research Center (NORC) in 1947, roughly two-thirds of Americans have consistently said that it would be better for the future of the United States to take an active role in world affairs. Around a quarter rejected that role. In the latest iteration of the question, 65 percent wanted the United States to take an active part, and 29 percent wanted the country to stay out (Gallup for the Chicago Council on Foreign Relations, October 1994). We are reluctant about becoming involved militarily abroad but also aware that military involvement cannot always be rejected. For the Japanese, the war and the impression made by the new Constitution produce more resistance to involvement.

Allies and Partners

Differences in orientations do not diminish feelings of solid ties between the United States and Japan. Since at least 1960, the Gallup Organization, in surveys for the Japanese Foreign Ministry, has asked Americans whether Japan is a dependable ally of the United States.

In 1960, 31 percent answered in the affirmative, and a majority, 55 percent, in the negative. In 1995, those numbers were reversed: 54 percent thought of Japan as a dependable ally, 33 percent did not (table 3–4). Majorities in Japan (in contemporary CBS/NYT/TBS polls) think that Japan would be a reliable ally of the United States. In December 1994, for example, 53 percent of the Japanese surveyed said Japan would be an ally the United States "can depend on"; 43 percent disagreed. Americans are even more certain that the United States would be an ally that Japan could depend on. Seventy-eight percent gave that response in December 1994 to the CBS/NYT/TBS group. (It should be noted that confidence about U.S. reliability appears to be deteriorating in Japan: 62 percent of the Japanese said the United States would be a reliable ally in 1990, 57 percent gave that response in 1991, and 47 percent answered that way in 1994.)

Surveys begun in Japan in 1956 (conducted by the United States Information Agency) asked the Japanese whether their nation should be on the side of the Communist powers, the anti-Communist powers, or on neither side.[7] In 1956, 46 percent of the Japanese surveyed said they sided with the free nations, 29 percent opted for neutrality, and 23 percent that they did not have an opinion. Only 2 percent sided with the Communist powers, the highest percentage ever recorded on this question. In 1994, in a Jiji Press question, 67 percent said they sided with the free world, fewer than 1 percent with the Communists. Still, 21 percent said that Japan should remain neutral, and 11 percent had no opinion.

When asked by the WSJ/NKS partnership in March 1995 whether each country would be an ally and partner on diplomatic and military issues or an adversary and competitor, majorities in Japan and in the United States said that in this area the other country would be an ally and partner. In the United States, nearly four in ten dissented; in Japan, only 23 percent did (table 3–5).

Military Activity

The strength of the relationship and the enormity of the change in attitudes since World War II can be seen in specific questions asked

---

7. The wording of this question and the sponsoring organizations have changed over time. In 1961, Jiji Press in Japan picked up the question asking about the free world, the Communist bloc, or neutrality. This organization has repeated the question many times since.

TABLE 3–4
ATTITUDES OF AMERICANS TOWARD JAPAN AS AN ALLY, 1960–1995
(percent)

Question: In your opinion, do you think Japan is or is not a dependable ally of the United States?

	Dependable	*Not Dependable*
1960	31	55
Feb. 1961	41	38
Sept. 1961	46	31
1962	46	33
1963	39	36
1964	44	33
1965	39	36
1966	42	35
1967	45	32
1968	40	34
1969	43	37
1970	44	36
1971	42	34
Mar. 1972	45	33
Nov. 1972	48	33
1974	36	37
Feb. 1975	49	31
Dec. 1975	49	39
1977	46	28
1978	53	23
1980	49	26
1982	53	23
1983	44	33
1984	57	24
1985	56	20
1986	55	22
1987	54	24
1988	48	30
1989	50	29
1990	44	40
1991	44	39
1992	49	42
1993	50	40
1994	43	43
1995	54	33

NOTE: Not all response categories are shown.
SOURCE: Surveys by the Gallup Organization for the Japanese Foreign Ministry, latest that of February 1995.

TABLE 3–5
PERCEPTIONS OF AMERICANS AND JAPANESE AS ALLIES OR ADVERSARIES, 1995
(percent)

Question: When it comes to (read item), do you see (Japan/U.S.) mostly as an ally and partner, or mostly as an adversary and competitor?

	Ally and Partner	Adversary and Competitor	Neither/ Both[a]	Not Sure
Americans				
Economic issues	19	76	2	3
Diplomatic and military issues	51	39	2	8
Japanese				
Economic issues	40	50	6	4
Diplomatic and military issues	60	23	9	8

a. Volunteered response.
SOURCE: Surveys by the *Wall Street Journal* (U.S.) and the *Nihon Keizai Shimbun* (Japan), March 1995.

about whether the United States would defend Japan if Japan were attacked. Because the Soviet threat has disappeared, pollsters have not asked as many questions as in the past about military adventurism. But from 1985 to 1991, CBS/NYT/TBS pollsters asked five times whether the United States would defend Japan if attacked. In each case, more than three-quarters of Americans said the United States would help Japan. In each asking of the question, the Japanese were less certain than the Americans that the United States would help (table 3–6). This uncertainty is long standing. In February 1970, when the Japanese were asked in a survey conducted by the Central Research Services whether they believed in the American promise to defend Japan, 30 percent said they did, 39 percent said they did not, and 31 percent had no opinion. Twenty-five years later, in the March 1995 WSJ/NKS poll, 76 percent of those surveyed in the United States said that the "United States could be counted on to come to the assistance of Japan if it faced military aggression." Sixteen percent disagreed. A near majority, 49 percent of the Japanese, felt confident of U.S. help, 38 percent did not (table 3–6).

TABLE 3–6
AMERICAN AND JAPANESE ATTITUDES TOWARD DEFENDING JAPAN, 1985–1995
(percent)

Question: If Japan were attacked, do you think the United States
would defend Japan, or do you think the United States would not
help Japan? (CBS/NYT/TBS) Do you think the United States could
be counted on to come to the assistance of Japan if it faced military
aggression? (WSJ/NKS)

	Would Defend	Would Not
Americans		
July 1985	79	8
May 1987	78	8
May 1988	78	10
Feb. 1989	77	8
Nov. 1991	84	4
March 1995	76	16
Japanese		
July 1985	42	54
May 1987	38	58
May 1988	45	50
Feb. 1989	44	46
Nov. 1991	58	40
March 1995	49	38

NOTE: Not all response categories are shown.
SOURCE: Surveys by CBS News/*New York Times* (U.S.) and the Tokyo Broad-
casting System (Japan), latest that of November 1991. Surveys by the *Wall
Street Journal* (U.S.) and the *Nihon Keizai Shimbun* (Japan), March 1995.

November 1991 and June 1993 surveys by the CBS/NYT/TBS
group found that 34 and 24 percent respectively of Japanese felt that
they had a responsibility "to give military assistance in trouble spots
around the world when it is asked by its allies," while strong majorities
(63 and 74 percent) said their country did not. The Japanese were
even divided about whether the Americans had this responsibility: 40
percent in 1993 said the United States did, but 57 percent said it did
not. In a question asked by this group in July 1985 and November
1991, slightly more than two in ten of the Japanese said that it was "not
very likely" that Japan would comply "if a situation developed where

the United States asked for military help from Japan." About two-thirds said it was somewhat likely that Japan would comply, but fewer than one in ten said it was "very" likely. (Americans were more confident of Japanese help than were the Japanese; 21 percent of them in 1985 and 18 percent in 1991 said such help was "very" likely).[8]

The issue of Japanese participation in UN peacekeeping operations underscores Japanese aversion to military involvement, but there is also evidence of a recognition in Japan of the need to participate more actively in the international community. A question asked in May 1993 by the Kyoto News Service illustrates. In it, 55 percent said Japanese participation in peacekeeping operations was unavoidable in order to contribute to the international community. Still, 32 percent said Japan should not participate. Only 8 percent favored active participation.

In June 1992, Japan enacted legislation that made Japanese Self-Defense Forces eligible to participate in UN peacekeeping operations. Surveys taken in Japan before the 1992 legislation showed that the Japanese opposed taking part in any activity that included a hint of military involvement. In one detailed question, asked in June 1991 by the *Asahi Shimbun,* only 17 percent said Japan should not take part at all in peacekeeping operations, 17 percent said they should take part carrying weapons, 12 percent said they should take part in monitoring cease-fires carrying weapons only for self-defense, but a strong plurality, 42 percent, said they should take part in nonmilitary actions monitoring elections.

A question asked by the *Asahi Shimbun* in November 1991 found 59 percent saying that having the Self-Defense Forces join the UN Peacekeeping Forces was "problematic." Twenty-seven percent said that it was not. A question posed by the *Yomiuri Shimbun* in March 1994 found the Japanese still split over whether the dispatch of Japan's Self-Defense Forces abroad "violated Japan's Constitution": 45 percent said that was closer to their view, 46 percent said that it did not violate the Constitution. A question asked five times between 1993 and 1995 by NHK shows that pluralities of the Japanese favor

---

8. The Japanese attitudes are not new, nor are they limited to assistance for the United States. In 1970, the Central Research Services polled the Japanese on whether Japan should give military aid to such Southeast Asian nations as Thailand, Laos, Cambodia, the Philippines, or Indonesia. Sixty percent said Japan should not, 34 percent said they did not have an opinion, and only 6 percent favored the idea. As for economic aid, there was slightly greater receptivity. Twenty-seven percent said it should be increased, 6 percent decreased, and 43 percent, kept level. A quarter had no opinion.

providing assistance that is short of military involvement. Only small numbers favor no Self-Defense Force involvement at all. In the latest of these, 25 percent told the NHK surveyors in March 1995 that Japan's Self-Defense Forces should participate in the peacekeeping operations, 23 percent that Japan should supervise cease-fire agreements without carrying weapons, 35 percent that Japan should not participate in any military actions but should provide medical and infrastructure support, and 6 percent said the Self-Defense Forces should not participate at all. The Japanese people appear to support the nation's recent participation in UN activities in Cambodia (monitoring elections) and in Rwanda (helping refugees).

Both the Japanese and the Americans feel that they have the responsibility to provide general economic assistance when asked by allies. Financial assistance to military peacekeeping efforts around the world is supported, though reservations are found in both countries. Fifty-four percent of the Japanese in a June 1993 CBS/NYT/TBS poll said that they had this responsibility; still, a significant 44 percent disagreed. In the United States, 55 percent felt Americans had this responsibility, 37 percent dissented.

Military Bases and the Security Treaty

A survey conducted by *Asahi Shimbun* in September 1950 found that 38 percent of the Japanese opposed continued U.S. military bases in Japan and that 30 percent favored them. In 1956, the United States Information Agency started asking the Japanese about the military bases. The identical question or a rough equivalent was asked in 1957, 1958, 1960, 1962, 1966, 1968, and 1970. In all but one asking of the question, majorities of the Japanese thought the bases were a bad idea for Japan. Around a third had no opinion, and fewer than 20 percent thought they were a good idea.[9] In a follow-up question asked in 1970 about why they thought the bases were a bad idea, "fear of war" was mentioned more often than any other reason, though the fact that many Japanese felt the bases were a nuisance followed closely behind. Far more Japanese thought the presence of the bases was a danger to their security than felt that they provided a guarantee of security.[10] Although the reasons may be different, the

9. Douglas H. Mendel, Jr., "Japan Reviews Her American Alliance," *Public Opinion Quarterly*, vol. 30, 1961, pp. 6–7; and "Japanese Views of the American Alliance in the Seventies," *Public Opinion Quarterly*, vol. 35, 1971, p. 530.
10. Ibid, p. 530.

Japanese remain averse to the stationing of U.S. troops on their soil. In the June 1990 CBS/NYT/TBS poll, Americans wanted to maintain the number of U.S. troops in Japan, but Japan wanted to see them decreased (47 percent) or eliminated (22 percent). Thirty-seven percent of Americans wanted them decreased or eliminated too.

In 1960, a majority of the Japanese did not have an opinion on the reauthorization of a revised United States-Japan Security Treaty. In 1970, for the first time, the Japanese could give a year's notice to terminate the treaty. With that change and others that had been made in the previous reauthorization, 39 percent endorsed the treaty's automatic continuation in a Central Research Services poll in February, 19 percent objected, and still a substantial 42 percent had no opinion.[11]

Another perspective on the treaty is provided by a question asked since 1969 by the Prime Minister's Office (table 3–7). In it, the Japanese are asked whether they want to see the treaty abolished, with Japan defending itself by its own forces; whether they wanted to maintain the treaty and defend Japan jointly; or whether they wanted to abolish the treaty and decrease or eliminate the Self-Defense Forces. In no instance have more than a handful of Japanese wanted to abolish the treaty and defend their nation themselves. Over the period, only small percentages have advocated abolishing the treaty and decreasing or eliminating the Self-Defense Forces. The plurality in 1969 who wanted to maintain the treaty has now become a solid majority (table 3–7). In June 1990 and November 1991, in the CBS/NYT/TBS collaboration, solid majorities of Americans also favored continuing the United States-Japan Security Treaty.

In September 1994, two-thirds of the Japanese surveyed by the *Yomiuri Shimbun* said that the treaty has a positive effect on Japan, though 19 percent disagreed (table 3–7). That question has been asked five other times since 1981, and in each survey, a plurality or a majority felt that the treaty has had a positive effect. In each of a half-dozen surveys taken by the Prime Minister's Office between 1978 and 1994, more than six in ten have consistently said the treaty had been useful for Japan. Fewer than 20 percent disagreed (table 3–7).

The kidnapping and rape of a Japanese schoolgirl by American servicemen stationed on Okinawa in September 1995 raised questions once again about the American military presence in Japan and about the continuation of the security treaty. A number of survey

---

11. Ibid, p. 527.

TABLE 3–7
ATTITUDES OF THE JAPANESE TOWARD THE U.S.-JAPAN
SECURITY TREATY, 1969–1994
(percent)

Question: What do you think should be done to maintain the peace and safety of Japan—abolish the U.S.-Japan Security Treaty and defend Japan with its own increased forces, maintain the U.S.-Japan Security Treaty and defend Japan with both the United States and the Self-Defense Forces, or abolish the U.S.-Japan Security Treaty and either decrease the offensive capacity of the Self-Defense Forces or eliminate the Forces entirely?

	Abolish Treaty and Defend Japan with Own Forces	Maintain Treaty and Defend Japan with U.S. and S.D.F.	Abolish Treaty and Decrease or Eliminate S.D.F.
1969	12	49	9
1971	10	40	15
1975	8	54	9
1978	8	61	5
1981	6	64	7
1984	5	69	6
1988	5	67	7
1991	7	62	10
1994	4	68	7

Question: Do you think the U.S.-Japan Security Treaty has a positive effect on Japan or not?

	Positive Effect	Not a Positive Effect
1981	55	13
1986	48	18
1988	53	18
1990	48	23
1991	50	23
1994	66	19

TABLE 3–7 (continued)

Question: How useful do you think the U.S.-Japan Security Treaty is in maintaining the peace and safety of Japan?

	Useful	*Not Useful*
1978	64	11
1981	65	12
1984	70	9
1988	68	11
1991	63	17
1994	68	14

NOTE: Not all response categories are shown.
SOURCES: For top and bottom panels, surveys by the Prime Minister's Office (Japan), latest that of 1994. For the middle panel, surveys by the *Yomiuri Shimbun*, latest that of 1994.

organizations went into the field to assess public feelings about the relationship. The surveys we reviewed showed support in both countries for the treaty but also, as we have seen before, a desire by the Japanese to have Americans reduce their military presence. The results from a joint Louis Harris and Associates and *Asahi Shimbun* poll illustrate. In late October 1995, 76 percent of Americans and 64 percent of Japanese said it was necessary for Japan and the United States "to maintain a security treaty." Nineteen percent of Americans and 21 percent of Japanese disagreed.

The October 1995 Gallup/*Yomiuri Shimbun* survey posed a four-part question about the treaty for American and Japanese respondents. Thirty percent of Americans said it is "definitely in the national interest to keep the treaty the same," 33 percent that it "may be" in the national interest to keep it the same, 15 percent that it may not be, and 6 percent that it definitely is not. Nineteen percent of Japanese said it is definitely in their national interest to keep the treaty, 38 percent that it may be, 15 percent that it may not be, and 8 percent that it definitely is not in Japan's interest. (Younger Japanese, under age thirty, were less likely than the population as a whole [44 to 57 percent] to say it is definitely or it may be in the national interest to maintain the treaty.) Of those in Japan who thought it may not or definitely is not in Japan's interest to maintain the treaty, more people cited crime by U.S. personnel, air pollution from the bases, and the concern that the treaty could lead to Japan's becoming involved in U.S. military operations than cited any other reasons for rethinking the treaty.

On the issue of troop presence, a huge majority of the Japanese (76 percent) wanted the United States to reduce its forces on the bases gradually, and 14 percent wanted the bases withdrawn immediately (Harris/*Asahi Shimbun*, October 1995). Seven percent wanted the bases maintained as they are now. The U.S. responses were: 41 percent, maintain the bases as they are now; 49 percent, reduce U.S. forces gradually; and 7 percent, withdraw all the bases immediately. The U.S. responses were similar to those the polling organizations found in 1992, when the same question was posed. The Japanese responses were somewhat different. In that year, 14 percent of the Japanese wanted to maintain the bases, 63 percent to reduce the forces on the bases gradually, and 18 percent to withdraw all the bases immediately. A broader question in the October 1995 Gallup/*Yomiuri Shimbun* survey found that 2 percent of the Japanese said the U.S. military presence in Asia should be increased, 33 percent that it should be maintained, and 57 percent that it should be decreased. A plurality of Americans (47 percent) wanted to maintain the U.S. presence, 32 percent to decrease it, and 8 percent to increase it. As we have said before, Japanese doubts about the U.S. troop presence are long standing.

On the issue of Japanese troop strength, five surveys for the CBS/NYT/TBS group between 1985 and 1991 showed that nearly six in ten of Japanese felt that it is at the right level. Majorities or pluralities of those surveyed in the United States agreed with the Japanese about it. Fewer than 24 percent in either country thought that Japan should increase its military strength. Gallup asks a question that has a different emphasis. It shows that between 1985 and 1989, a plurality of Americans felt that Japan should increase its military forces for its own defense. From 1990 to the present, a plurality or majority have said Japan should not. Twenty-eight percent in February 1995 said Japan should increase its military forces for its own defense, and 61 percent said it should not (table 3–8).

In both countries, the military seems to be highly respected, although the Japanese see its role differently. In a 1994 survey for the Prime Minister's Office, 77 percent had a good image of the military, with only 13 percent unfavorable. In the eight other iterations of this question asked since 1969, strong majorities have always had a good image. The Japanese see its future role as first helping out in natural disasters and then in defense. The U.S. military is the most highly

TABLE 3–8
AMERICAN AND JAPANESE ATTITUDES TOWARD INCREASING JAPANESE
ARMED FORCES, 1985–1995
(percent)

Question: Do you feel Japan should further increase its military forces for its own defense or not?

	Increase	Not Increase	No Opinion
Americans			
Jan. 1985	46	27	27
Jan. 1986	42	26	32
Jan. 1987	40	33	27
Jan. 1988	37	35	28
Jan. 1989	39	38	23
Feb. 1990	36	45	19
Jan. 1991	39	43	18
Feb. 1992	39	55	6
Feb. 1993	47	47	6
Feb. 1994	33	58	9
Feb. 1995	28	61	11

Question: Do you think Japan should increase its military strength, decrease its military strength, or do you think its current military strength is at the right level?

	Increase	Decrease	Right Level
Americans			
July 1985	18	6	54
May 1987	12	8	44
May 1988	24	7	46
Feb. 1989	18	8	48
Nov. 1991	17	10	52
Japanese			
July 1985	11	25	59
May 1987	10	28	59
May 1988	9	29	58
Feb. 1989	10	31	57
Nov. 1991	7	32	59

NOTE: For bottom panel, not all response categories are shown.
SOURCES: For top panel, surveys by the Gallup Organization for the Japan Information Center, latest that of February 1995. For bottom panel, surveys by CBS News/New York Times (U.S.) and Tokyo Broadcasting System (Japan), latest that of November 1991.

regarded institution in the United States. A 1995 Louis Harris and Associates question found that more Americans had a great deal of confidence in those running the military than had such confidence in any other of eleven institutions the survey organization inquired about.

An issue related to military readiness is nuclear capability, and the subject has received attention in Japan from the press and pollsters. China's decision to conduct an underground nuclear test in May 1995 brought the issue to the surface again. In July 1985 and July 1995, about two in ten Japanese told CBS/NYT/TBS interviewers that Japan has its own nuclear weapons; three-quarters said it does not. Only a small percentage of those who felt Japan does not have nuclear weapons felt the country would have them in the near future. In the 1985 survey, more than eight in ten Japanese said their nation should not have nuclear weapons. The results from the March 1995 WSJ/NKS survey reinforce this opposition. Only 11 percent of the Japanese surveyed said Japan would acquire nuclear weapons in the next ten years. Eighty-six percent said their country would not.

Looking Ahead

Japan has been wrestling for some time now with questions about the role it will play internationally. Seventy-two percent of Japanese respondents in the March 1995 WSJ/NKS poll answered the general question about whether the country should become more active in world affairs by saying that Japan should become more active, 2 percent said less active, and 23 percent felt that Japan should continue its current level of activity. Still, slightly more than four in ten respondents in surveys conducted in June 1993 and December 1994 in Japan by the CBS/NYT/TBS group felt that if Japan increased its military power to become involved in international peacekeeping operations, there would be a danger of the country's becoming too aggressive. (A 54 percent majority dissented in both surveys.)

Americans are very much aware of the international role they must play, though they are weary of having to carry such a burden and often cranky about its costs. Reflecting these feelings, 47 percent in the same WSJ/NKS survey said the United States should maintain its current level of activity in world affairs, 34 percent said we should be less active, and 17 percent more active.

The contrasting orientations have produced and will continue to produce frictions in the relationship of the kind we saw during the Vietnam and Persian Gulf wars. These must be understood in the context of substantial areas of agreement. There is little evidence that the frictions will cause a fracturing of the military and diplomatic relationship. When asked which one or two of the following characteristics are the most impressive features of the United States in the March 1995 WSJ/NKS poll, more people in both countries said "its leadership role in foreign affairs" than mentioned other defining or admired characteristics, such as its political system or its technological achievements. In another question in this survey, 69 percent of the Japanese and 76 percent of the Americans expected the United States and Japan to be allies in twenty years. Only small numbers (15 percent in the United States, 18 percent in Japan) disagreed.

While Americans have been and will in the future be critical of Japan in this sphere (and vice versa), there is substantial goodwill in the relationship. In the February 1995 Gallup survey for the Japan Information Center, 67 percent of Americans described post–World War II relations between the United States and Japan as positive (11 percent very positive, 56 somewhat positive), and 28 percent described them as negative (22 somewhat, 6 percent very). Looking ahead, as Americans were asked to do in the Chicago Council on Foreign Relations October 1994 poll, more of them felt that the United States had a vital interest in Japan than felt that way about any other nation the surveyors mentioned.

Economic Relations

If, despite the experience of a war and a peace that produced substantially different orientations, there is substantial goodwill in international relations today, the same cannot be said about trade relations between the two superpowers. The June 1995 CBS/TBS survey conducted at the time of intense negotiations over a 100-percent luxury tariff on Japanese cars sold in the United States found the highest number of Americans and the second-highest number of Japanese saying that relations between the two countries are unfriendly in the ten-year history of the poll—certainly not an auspicious sign for the future.

But we must ask whether trade frictions that are evident in surveys bespeak a fundamental and permanent deterioration in popular perceptions of U.S.-Japanese relations. The answer requires putting current controversies into perspective by examining general attitudes about trade.

A question cited in the last section of this report from the March 1995 WSJ/NKS poll found that majorities in Japan and in the United States saw each other as allies and partners in diplomatic and military terms, but that 76 percent of U.S. respondents saw Japan as more of an adversary and competitor in economic relations (19 percent saw it as an ally and partner). Fifty percent of the Japanese saw the United States as an economic adversary or competitor, and 40 percent as an ally or partner (table 3–5). In the same survey, 70 percent of U.S. respondents named Japan as their country's biggest competitor, and 40 percent of the Japanese returned the compliment. (In this poll as in other recent ones, Japanese concern about China as a major competitor is evident. Thirty-five percent in this question named China as their country's biggest competitor. A more recent October 1995 Gallup/*Yomiuri Shimbun* survey found 32 percent of Japanese naming the United States as their most formidable future economic competitor, and 34 percent China.) In the Gallup/Chicago Council study in 1994, 62 percent of respondents surveyed in the United States said that economic competition from Japan was a critical threat to the United States. Still, other concerns, such as the threat of certain countries acquiring nuclear capability, the growing number of immigrants, and international terrorism, were thought to be greater problems.

These numbers must be seen in perspective. Even in the most difficult periods, neither trade nor competition with Japan has ever been mentioned by more than a handful of American respondents as the most important problem facing the United States. In the eight CBS/NYT surveys in 1994 that asked about the "most important problem" facing the country, trade has never been mentioned by more than 1 percent of those surveyed. Foreign policy was mentioned by 6 percent in one survey. In the January 1996 survey, the pollsters recorded mentions of seventeen different issues as each being the most important problem facing the country. Neither Japan nor trade was among them. (The deficit was the number one concern, cited by 19 percent of those surveyed.) In past years, relations with the former Soviets made the list, as did the war in the Persian Gulf. When the Chicago Council on Foreign Relations asked Americans the more specific question about the "two or three biggest foreign policy problems" facing the United States today, 8 percent mentioned international trade. So for most Americans most of the time, trade frictions with Japan are not central issues.

Sustained attention was given to the ratification of the North American Free Trade Agreement (NAFTA) in 1993. The polls conducted at the time in the United States reflected the same public ambivalence about trade issues that we find in the data about U.S.-Japanese relations, but the proximity of Mexico and the problem of immigration suggested to many observers that the issue had the potential to become more potent in elections. At the time of the debate, many politicians, including Ross Perot, and union leaders predicted that a vote in favor of the agreement would have significant negative electoral consequences. An October 1994 district-by-district election analysis by the *Wall Street Journal*, however, found that the "threat to dethrone NAFTA backers . . . has ended up looking hollow." Beyond this assessment, the exit-polling consortium called the Voter News Service, comprising the four networks and the Associated Press, inquired on election day about NAFTA in Ohio and Texas. In Ohio, 26 percent of voters said it had helped their state, 23 percent said it had hurt, and a third said it had had no effect. In Texas, 39 percent said the agreement had helped, 16 percent that it had hurt, and 30 percent that it had had no effect. It is hard to find many examples of state or local elections where trade issues have had any significant effect on electoral outcomes, though politicians in both parties have tried to use problems in the U.S.-Japanese relationship to gain political advantage.

General Attitudes about Trade

The polls have long shown that at one level, Americans and Japanese favor import protection even if it means they will have fewer choices. In three separate surveys in the CBS/NYT/TBS polls, majorities (56 percent in May 1988, 54 percent in June/July 1989, and 51 percent in June 1990) felt that the idea that "trade restrictions are necessary to protect domestic industries" came closer to their opinion. Thirty-four, 36, and 39 percent, respectively, chose the response of "free trade must be allowed, even if domestic industries are hurt by foreign competition." Japanese sentiments were remarkably similar (59 versus 34 percent in 1988, 62 versus 35 percent in 1989, and 57 versus 40 percent in 1990).

On the emotional issue of protecting farmers, 74 percent in Japan in the May 1988 survey and 57 percent in the United States felt that restrictions on the import of agricultural products were needed to protect domestic farmers. Forty percent in Japan and 21 percent in the United States opted for no restrictions. When asked specifically about importing rice from the United States, more than six in ten Japanese respondents in the CBS/NYT/TBS poll said that Japan should not import rice even if that made it possible to buy rice more

41

cheaply. Still, attitudes appear to be softening a bit in Japan on the issue. In a March 1994 NHK poll that specified that GATT was requiring Japan to open its rice market, 65 percent said that the country "can't help but open it to some extent." Only 18 percent said it should not be opened at all. In the NHK poll, 14 percent said that the rice market should never be liberalized, 60 percent that it was "necessary to liberalize partly, but farmers must be protected somehow," and 21 percent wanted to encourage further liberalization to ensure free trade.

People in both countries think a free and open trading system is desirable. A WSJ/NKS poll from March 1995 found that an identical 23 percent in both countries felt that "restricting imports to save jobs" was the more important goal, while 72 percent in the United States and 63 percent in Japan thought that "expanding exports to create jobs" was. And there is the realization that countries gain competitive advantage from the strength of their products. In surveys in February 1987 and May 1989 by Yankelovich Clancy Shulman, more than six in ten surveyed in the United States said "the Japanese are successful in world trade because they produce quality products for a good price." Slightly more than two in ten in each survey said they were successful because they engage in unfair trade practices.

Since 1985, the CBS/NYT/TBS group has been asking Americans and Japanese whether, on balance, trading with Japan, both buying and selling products, is good or bad for the U.S. or Japanese economies. Perhaps reflecting generally more positive views about the U.S. competitive position recently, a strong plurality in the United States in 1993, a majority in 1994, and a plurality again in June 1995 felt that trade with Japan is good for the United States. When the question was first asked in 1985, 35 percent of U.S. respondents answered in the affirmative (table 3–9). Majorities or pluralities of the Japanese (in a separate question) felt that trade with Japan is good for the United States.

Perhaps reflecting current pessimism in Japan about its economy, a decreasing number there have felt that trade with the United States is good for the Japanese economy. Still, in June 1995, 47 percent felt that way (down from 63 percent in 1989), 17 percent said it is bad, and 31 percent that it has no effect (table 3–9).

Between 1985 and 1995, CBS/NYT/TBS surveyors asked Americans and Japanese how much Japan restricts the sale of American goods in Japan. The number of Americans who said that Japan restricts these sales "a great deal" increased 16 percentage points

TABLE 3–9

U.S. AND JAPANESE ATTITUDES TOWARD THE TRADE BALANCE,
1985–1995
(percent)

Question: On balance, do you think trade with (Japan/U.S.)—both buying and selling products—is good for the (U.S./Japanese) economy, or
is it bad for the (U.S./Japanese) economy, or does it have no effect?

Trade with Japan	Is Good for the U.S. Economy	Is Bad	No Effect
Americans			
July 1985	35	48	7
Apr. 1986	37	45	7
May 1987	37	44	7
May 1988	42	41	6
Feb. 1989	34	40	11
Dec. 1992	42	44	7
June 1993	46	40	10
Dec. 1994	51	32	13
June 1995	45	40	6

Trade with the United States	Is Good for the Japanese Economy	Is Bad	No Effect
Japanese			
May 1987	42	23	28
May 1988	46	19	30
Feb. 1989	63	11	21
Dec. 1992	53	7	38
June 1993	59	8	32
Dec. 1994	42	7	28
June 1995	47	17	31

NOTE: Not all response categories are shown.
SOURCE: Surveys by CBS News/*New York Times* (U.S.) and the Tokyo Broadcasting System (Japan), latest that of June 1995.

over that decade. In 1995, a near majority gave that response. In
Japan roughly two in ten see their government as restricting American products a great deal, but a majority has consistently said the government does this "some" (table 3–10).

43

TABLE 3–10
U.S. AND JAPANESE ATTITUDES TOWARD JAPAN'S RESTRICTIONS ON
AMERICAN GOODS, 1985–1995
(percent)

Question: How much do you think Japan's government now restricts the sale of American goods in Japan—a great deal, some, not much, or not at all?

	A Great Deal	Some	Not Much	Not at All
Americans				
July 1985	32	42	9	4
April 1986	33	40	10	3
May 1987	36	22	12	4
May 1988	44	33	9	2
June 1989	42	35	8	2
June 1995	48	33	7	2
Japanese				
July 1985	20	50	22	10
April 1986	20	53	20	2
May 1987	22	54	19	1
May 1988	24	55	17	1
June 1989	18	65	14	2
June 1995	14	53	23	2

NOTE: Not all response categories are shown.
SOURCE: Surveys by CBS News/New York Times (U.S.) and Tokyo Broadcasting System (Japan), latest that of June 1995.

In the poll, a question about U.S. government practices was not asked as often. The Japanese were more likely than the Americans to say in May of 1987 and 1988 that the U.S. government restricts the sale of Japanese goods in the United States. (Sixty-three percent of Japanese in 1987, 67 percent in 1988, and 47 percent of Americans in both years thought the U.S. government restricts the sale of Japanese goods in the United States "a great deal" or "some".)

Over the years, the CBS/NYT/TBS polling group has asked both peoples whether Japanese companies are competing unfairly or whether the United States is blaming Japan for its own economic problems. More Americans in the 1990s than in the 1980s believe

TABLE 3–11

U.S. AND JAPANESE ATTITUDES TOWARD COMPLAINTS ABOUT UNFAIR
TRADE, 1985–1994

(percent)

Question: Which of the following statements comes closer to your
opinion—Japanese companies are competing unfairly with American companies, or the United States is blaming Japan for its own economic problems?

	Japanese Companies Are Competing Unfairly	United States Is Blaming Japan for Its Own Economic Problems
Americans		
July 1985	30	53
May 1987	34	49
May 1988	33	48
June 1990	38	44
Nov. 1991	32	47
Dec. 1992	40	49
June 1993	45	44
Dec. 1994	40	47
Japanese		
July 1985	19	70
May 1987	16	77
May 1988	19	73
June 1990	26	68
Nov. 1991	21	76
Dec. 1992	17	78
June 1993	12	85
Dec. 1994	18	79

NOTE: Not all response categories are shown.
SOURCE: Surveys by CBS News/*New York Times* (U.S.) and the Tokyo Broadcasting System (Japan), latest that of December 1994.

that Japan is competing unfairly (table 3–11), but more than four in
ten have consistently said that the United States is blaming Japan
unfairly. In a June 1995 survey, in a broader question, 34 percent of
Americans said the United States is more to blame for current trade
problems, and 46 percent said Japan is. In Japan, 29 percent said the

United States is more to blame, 22 percent said the Japanese are, and 42 percent volunteered that both are to blame.

Respondents in both countries are willing to accept at least some of the blame for trade tensions. In an October 1994 Japanese survey conducted for the Prime Minister's Office, 30 percent of the Japanese respondents said the U.S. response to trade frictions is "understandable," while slightly more than four in ten called it "emotional." In the late 1980s and early 1990s, in seven different surveys, roughly three in ten (the number reached 37 percent) felt that the U.S. response is understandable. In a broader question asked by the *Asahi Shimbun* in May 1994, 36 percent of Japanese respondents felt that Japan "should be blamed more for not being able to solve the longstanding economic problems between the two countries," and a virtually identical number felt the United States deserved more of the blame. In the October 1995 Gallup/*Yomiuri Shimbun* survey, 53 percent in the United States and 66 percent in Japan said both countries are equally responsible for the frictions in economic matters. Thirty-two percent of Americans said Japan is mainly responsible (up from 12 percent in 1991). Twenty percent of the Japanese said the United States is mainly responsible.

Individuals in both countries have been asked a number of times by the CBS/NYT/TBS pollsters whether the trade situation between the United States and Japan had changed their feeling about the other country. In 1985, 1987, 1988, and 1989, 79 percent, 75 percent, 72 percent, and 62 percent in the United States said their feelings had not changed. Thirteen, 17, 17, and 26 percent said that their feelings had changed, and that they felt less friendly. In Japan, similarly substantial majorities (79 percent in 1985, 78 percent in 1987, 78 percent in 1988, and 76 percent in 1989) said their feelings had not changed. Fewer than 20 percent said that their feelings had changed for the worse. A May 1987 CBS/NYT/TBS survey found that 46 percent of Americans admired Japan for selling more to the United States than the United States sells to Japan. Twenty percent felt angry about it. In the June 1995 CBS/NYT/TBS poll, 35 percent of Americans said the recent trade problems had changed their attitudes about buying Japanese products; 62 percent said their attitudes had not been changed.

In the discussion above, we have tried to highlight questions that tap into fundamental aspects of the economic relationship. We have avoided those questions that ask people to speculate about future economic relations, though many such questions are regularly asked by pollsters in both countries. The results of these questions are often unstable—they vary significantly from survey organization to organization, and even within a single organization's poll, depending on slight changes in wording and timing. The questions are often asked when trade negotiations are front-page news, and responses at those times can reflect the passions of the moment and not some fundamental change in the relationship. But more important, we believe that questions asked about the present are more reliable and revealing than those that ask people to speculate about the future.

We have not dwelt on the question of which country will be the number one economic power in the future, though this question seems to produce many headlines here and abroad. Suffice it to say there is concern in Japan today about its future, based on pessimism about its current economic situation. In the United States, we are a bit more optimistic about our competitive position than we were in the late 1980s and early 1990s, when the "declinism" so fashionable among elites crept into public opinion data. There is enough confusion in the data about the present state of our relationship without focusing on these other concerns. We turn now to general assessment of present-day relations.

General Evaluations

How are we to sum up the health of the U.S.-Japanese relationship today? Have the foreign policy or economic frictions of late caused anything fundamental about the relationship to change? Do the differences in international orientations portend a significant undermining of the general commitment we have to each other? These are big questions, of course, and particularly ambitious ones for two authors not schooled in Japanese political life or culture. But the polls do provide much information from which we can draw some general conclusions.

Majorities in Japan and the United States describe U.S.-Japanese relations since World War II as positive. A more specific question asked in both Japan and the United States by Gallup and the *Yomiuri Shimbun* in September 1994 found that majorities of the Japanese, and less strong pluralities or majorities of the Americans, had positive impressions of four different areas where we interact—trade, cooperation in security policy, exchanges, and cooperation in science and technology (table 3–12).

Beyond this, a whole slew of surveys in both countries show that Americans rank Japan highly. In the Jiji Press surveys conducted regu-

TABLE 3–12
U.S. AND JAPANESE ATTITUDES TOWARD POST–WORLD WAR II
RELATIONS, 1994
(percent)

Question: What do you think about each of the following aspects of
post–World War II relations between Japan and the United States?

	Positive	Negative
Americans		
Trade	48	41
Cooperation in security policy	45	33
Exchanges of adults/students	69	14
Cooperation in science and technology	52	31
Japanese		
Trade	79	15
Cooperation in security policy	72	17
Exchanges of adults/students	79	11
Cooperation in science and technology	86	7

NOTE: Not all response categories are shown.
SOURCE: Survey by the Gallup Organization and the *Yomiuri Shimbun*, September 1994.

larly since 1961, the United States, Switzerland, and England have
ranked higher than any other nations (including France, India, China,
the Republic of Korea, and the former Soviet Union) as countries
most liked. Only a handful in this survey (usually fewer than 10 percent) have ever labeled the United States as the country most disliked
(table 3–13). In the Gallup-*Yomiuri Shimbun* surveys conducted since
1979, Japan has not ranked as high as Canada, England, or Australia
in Americans' eyes as the most trustworthy nation, but it has usually
fallen into a group of countries such as Mexico, united Germany, Italy,
New Zealand, and Israel. Each time the survey partnership has asked
the Japanese about the United States since 1984, the United States has
ranked higher than any other nation as most trustworthy.

The Chicago Council of Foreign Relations has Americans picture
a thermometer and then asks how warm their feelings are toward various countries. In October 1994, U.S. respondents rated Canada (73
degrees) and Great Britain (69 degrees) most warmly. Japan ranked
in the middle of the 50s, with Italy, Germany, Mexico, France, Russia,

TABLE 3–13
POSITIVE AND NEGATIVE JAPANESE ATTITUDES TOWARD VARIOUS COUNTRIES, 1982–1994
(percent)

Question: What countries do you like? Choose up to three from the list.

	United States[a]	France	China
January 1982	38	22	16
January 1983	37	24	18
January 1984	42	26	20
January 1985	45	26	24
January 1986	43	26	24
January 1987	39	25	21
January 1988	41	24	23
January 1989	43	27	19
January 1990	45	31	6
January 1991	43	29	9
January 1992	44	27	12
January 1993	45	31	13
January 1994	43	30	15

Question: What countries do you dislike? Choose up to three from the list.

	United States	Russia	China
January 1982	5	51	5
January 1983	7	49	5
January 1984	5	61	5
January 1985	5	57	5
January 1986	5	51	3
January 1987	7	51	4
January 1988	6	51	6
January 1989	4	41	4
January 1990	5	40	23
January 1991	6	33	13
January 1992	7	33	14
January 1993	6	44	10
January 1994	6	52	11

a. In every year, Switzerland (not shown in this chart) was listed side-by-side with the United States as the top choice.
SOURCE: Surveys by the Jiji Press, latest that of January 1994.

Israel, Brazil, Poland, and South Africa. Surveys taken between 1985 and 1995 in Japan for the Prime Minister's Office find that solid majorities of Japanese say they have an affinity with the United States, with only about 20 percent saying they have no affinity. Other surveys consistently show that we rank very highly in each other's estimation on broad comparative measures of likability and trustworthiness.

These general positive impressions are supported by other survey data. More than three-quarters of Americans have consistently described their personal feelings toward Japan as friendly in the ten years the CBS/NYT/TBS group has been asking the question. The organization changed the wording of the question it used in Japan, but in the late 1980s and early 1990s, solid majorities of Japanese said they felt friendly toward the United States. More recently, with the new question wording, significant numbers of Japanese have responded "neither" (table 3–14). Surveys taken by the *Asahi Shimbun* in the late 1980s and early 1990s confirm that majorities of the Japanese choose the "neither" response when offered it, but still, in these surveys and in the CBS/NYT/TBS ones, the number who feel friendly exceeds the number who feel unfriendly.

In Gallup surveys in the United States, the number saying they had a favorable opinion of Japan has dropped since 1978 when the question was first asked, but still, in 1994, a majority (54 percent) had a positive impression (table 3–15). Japan is viewed more favorably than China. Surveys conducted by the National Opinion Research Center also find a drop in those rating Japan favorably since 1974, when the question was first asked, but again, a solid majority rates the country positively (table 3–16).

These questions and the next group suggest that the frictions in trade and military relations have taken some toll on the relationship. Still, the data are ambiguous. Since 1990, the Prime Minister's Office has asked the Japanese yearly whether relations between Japan and the United States are sound ("sound" or "basically sound, although there are problems") or unsound ("deteriorating considerably" and "in a dangerous condition"). In 1994, 65 percent described relations as sound, 26 unsound. Only 2 percent (of the 26 percent who said unsound) described them as being in a dangerous condition. A survey conducted in Japan since 1978 by the Prime Minister's Office found that in 1994, 72 percent of the Japanese surveyed said they felt strongly or somewhat strongly tied to the United States. The percentage was the same in 1978 (table 3–17).

TABLE 3–14
FRIENDLINESS OF FEELING BETWEEN AMERICANS AND JAPANESE, 1985–1994
(percent)

Question: Overall, are your feelings toward (Japan/U.S.) generally friendly, or generally unfriendly?

	Friendly	Unfriendly	Neither
Americans			
July 1985	87	8	NA
May 1987	75	16	NA
May 1988	76	15	NA
Feb. 1989	73	18	NA
June 1989	74	19	NA
Jan. 1990	67	25	NA
June 1990	75	18	NA
Nov. 1991	77	17	NA
Dec. 1992	73	19	NA
June 1993	72	21	NA
Dec. 1994	78	16	NA
	Friendly	Unfriendly	Neither
Japanese			
May 1987	33	13	52
May 1988	65	32	NA
Feb. 1989	70	26	NA
June 1989	57	18	NA
June 1990	66	30	NA
Nov. 1991	65	33	NA
Dec. 1992	28	16	56
June 1993	26	19	55
Dec. 1994	26	13	61

NOTE: Between May 1988 and November 1991, the Japanese did not give respondents the "neither" category. The Americans did not offer the "neither" category at all. Not all response categories are shown.
SOURCE: Surveys by CBS News/*New York Times* (U.S.) and the Tokyo Broadcasting System (Japan), latest that of December 1994 (U.S.) and November 1991 (Japan).

TABLE 3–15

AMERICANS' OPINIONS OF JAPAN AND CHINA, 1978–1994 AND 1967–1994
(percent)

Question: Now, I'd like your overall opinion of some foreign countries. First, is your overall opinion of [country]—very favorable, mostly favorable, mostly unfavorable, or very unfavorable? Next, what is your overall opinion of [country]...?

	Very Favorable	Mostly Favorable	Mostly Unfavorable	Very Unfavorable
Japan				
Apr. 1978	23	50	13	4
Sept. 1979	32	50	8	4
Dec. 1987	21	51	15	6
Mar. 1989	12	57	16	7
Aug. 1989	10	48	23	10
Feb. 1991	11	51	21	9
Mar. 1991	10	55	19	7
Nov. 1991	7	41	29	12
Feb. 1992	9	38	28	22
June 1993	7	41	30	16
July 1993	7	41	30	16
Feb. 1994	7	47	28	14
China				
1967	a	5	16	75
Jan. 1976	3	17	29	45
Feb. 1979	5	25	31	33
Jan. 1980	6	36	30	24
Sept. 1983	6	37	31	21
May 1987	8	57	23	5
Feb. 1989	12	60	10	3
July 1989	5	29	32	22
Nov. 1993	10	43	24	15
Feb. 1994	4	36	38	15

NOTE: Not all response categories are shown.
a. Less than 0.5.
SOURCE: Surveys by the Gallup Organization, latest that of February 1994.

TABLE 3–16
AMERICANS' LIKE AND DISLIKE OF JAPAN, 1974–1994
(percent)

Question: You will notice that the boxes on this card go from the highest position of "plus 5" for a country which you like very much, to the lowest position of "minus 5" for a country you dislike very much. How far up the scale or how far down the scale would you rate Japan?

	+5,+4	+3,+2,+1	−1,−2,−3	−4,−5
1974	17	53	15	10
1975	15	51	18	9
1977	14	49	18	10
1982	17	50	19	10
1983	15	51	21	9
1985	18	51	20	7
1986	18	55	16	7
1988	16	52	19	9
1989	17	51	18	10
1990	16	48	19	13
1991	18	46	17	13
1993	14	47	21	13
1994	15	43	23	14

NOTE: Not all response categories are shown.
SOURCE: Surveys by the National Opinion Research Center, latest that of January–May 1994.

The CBS/NYT/TBS polls in the United States since 1985 show a drop in the number describing relations as friendly. Still, in June 1995, 60 percent described them that way, while 36 percent described them as unfriendly. Japanese feelings about relations have been much more volatile over the ten-year history of the poll, and they have dropped more sharply. In June 1995 they reached the lowest point ever recorded in the survey. The 1987 and 1995 polls that show very sharp erosion in positive Japanese feelings about the relationship were taken at times of intense trade frictions—over semiconductors in 1987 and over the luxury tariff on autos in 1995 (table 3–18).

The surveys conducted over the years by Louis Harris and Associates and the *Asahi Shimbun* find more Japanese saying relations are

TABLE 3–17
JAPANESE FEELINGS OF CLOSENESS TO VARIOUS COUNTRIES, 1978–1994
(percent)

Question: To what degree do you feel tied to the following nations?

	United States	Russia	China	European Union[a]
1978	72	11	61	—
1979	77	12	70	—
1980	76	8	77	—
1981	69	7	68	—
1982	71	8	72	—
1983	71	8	71	—
1984	74	7	74	—
1985	75	8	75	—
1986	66	9	68	—
1987	72	9	68	—
1988	73	14	68	—
1989	76	12	52	—
1990	74	22	52	47
1991	77	24	50	46
1992	73	14	55	45
1993	75	10	53	48
1994	72	11	51	46

a. European Union not in existence before 1990.
SOURCE: Surveys by the Prime Minister's Office, latest that of 1994.

not good than good (50 percent as compared with 29 percent, in October 1995). The "good" responses have shown considerable volatility. In the United States, Harris frames the question differently, asking whether relations are, alternately, excellent/pretty good or only fair/poor. Positive feelings have dropped since the question was first asked in 1982 (table 3–19).

The Gallup/*Yomiuri Shimbun* polls show a drop since 1979, using the "very good/good" and "just fair/poor" formulation, from 57 percent positive in the United States in 1979 to only 28 percent positive in October 1995. Japanese responses show a drop, too. In 1995, 23 percent of the Japanese described relations as very good or good and 72 percent as just fair or poor (table 3–20). A question asked by the Prime Minister's Office in 1988 and 1995 shows hardly any deterio-

TABLE 3–18
U.S. AND JAPANESE PERCEPTIONS OF FRIENDLINESS OF RELATIONS WITH
THE OTHER COUNTRY, 1985–1995
(percent)

Question: How would you describe relations between Japan and the
United States today? Would you say relations are very friendly, somewhat friendly, somewhat unfriendly, or very unfriendly?

	Friendly	*Unfriendly*
Americans		
July 1985	88	7
Apr. 1986	85	8
May 1987	72	19
May 1988	73	17
Feb. 1989	79	12
June 1989	80	16
June 1990	84	12
Nov. 1991	80	15
Dec. 1992	77	17
June 1993	70	25
Dec. 1994	79	18
June 1995	60	36
Japanese		
July 1985	73	21
Apr. 1986	66	29
May 1987	43	55
May 1988	54	43
Feb. 1989	68	29
June 1989	67	32
June 1990	63	36
Nov. 1991	60	39
Dec. 1992	53	46
June 1993	35	64
Dec. 1994	50	49
June 1995	39	60

NOTE: "Friendly" = "very friendly" plus "somewhat friendly"; "unfriendly" =
"somewhat unfriendly" plus "very unfriendly."
Not all response categories are shown.
SOURCE: Surveys by CBS News/*New York Times* (U.S.) and the Tokyo Broadcasting System (Japan), latest that of June 1995.

TABLE 3–19
U.S. AND JAPANESE PERCEPTIONS OF CURRENT RELATIONS, PART I, 1982–1995
(percent)

Question: How would you rate the present relations between the
United States and Japan—excellent, pretty good, only fair, or poor?

	Excellent/ Pretty Good	Only Fair/ Poor	Not Sure
Americans			
Mar. 1982	61	37	2
Oct. 1986	64	33	3
May 1987	47	51	2
Dec. 1988	56	39	4
Feb. 1991	66	30	4
June 1991	51	40	8
Nov. 1991	61	38	1
Dec. 1992	38	59	3
Dec. 1993	49	49	2
May 1994	40	56	4
Oct. 1995	34	62	4

Question: Do you think that present relations between the United
States and Japan are good, or not?

	Are Good	Are Not Good	Can't Say
Japanese			
Mar. 1982	32	45	17
Oct. 1986	48	30	14
May 1987	36	37	18
Dec. 1988	38	37	16
Feb. 1991	48	28	16
June 1991	37	41	18
Nov. 1991	39	37	18
Dec. 1992	30	47	16
Dec. 1993	37	42	15
Feb. 1994	20	64	11
May 1994	30	57	6
Nov. 1994	27	48	19
Oct. 1995	29	50	15

NOTE: In top panel, percentages may not add to 100 because of rounding.
In bottom panel, not all response categories are shown.
SOURCE: Surveys by Louis Harris and Associates and the *Asahi Shimbun*, lat-
est that of October 1995.

TABLE 3–20
U.S. AND JAPANESE PERCEPTIONS OF CURRENT RELATIONS, PART II,
1979–1995
(percent)

Question: Do you think that relations between the United States and Japan are very good, good, just fair, or poor at present?

	Very Good/Good	Just Fair/Poor
Americans		
1979	57	35
1982	47	45
1983	64	31
1984	59	35
1985	60	34
1986	60	35
1987	48	46
1988	48	45
1989	46	49
1990	49	47
1991	42	51
1992	26	69
1993	37	54
1994	32	59
1995	28	65
Japanese		
1979	48	43
1982	33	58
1983	48	44
1984	53	40
1985	41	52
1986	42	49
1987	33	61
1988	42	53
1989	38	55
1990	43	53
1991	41	57
1992	30	66
1994	35	60
1995	23	72

NOTE: Not all response categories are shown.
SOURCE: Surveys by the Gallup Organization and the *Yomiuri Shimbun*, latest that of October–November, 1995 (U.S.) and October 1995 (Japan).

TABLE 3–21

LABELS CHOSEN BY AMERICANS AND JAPANESE TO CHARACTERIZE THE
RELATIONSHIP OF THE TWO COUNTRIES, 1994

(percent)

Question: Please choose the one word from the list which best completes this sentence: To (Japan/U.S.), the (U.S./Japan) is like a. . . .

	Americans	Japanese
Rival	52	27
Friend	19	38
Enemy	5	3
Parent	2	10
Elder brother	1	10
Teacher	6	5
Younger brother	4	*
Student	1	*

NOTE: Not all response categories are shown. Asterisks indicate responses of less than 1 percent.
SOURCE: Survey by the Gallup Organization and the *Yomiuri Shimbun*, September–October 1994 (U.S.) and September 1994 (Japan).

ration in the percentage of the Japanese saying the relationship between the United States and Japan is good. Sixty-three percent gave that response in 1995.

People with differences can still be good friends, of course. Economic rivals can see important long-term benefits in the relationship. Table 3–21 shows that U.S. respondents are more likely to view Japan as a rival than as a friend, and that more Japanese say friend than rival.

How then would we summarize the data about the way we see each other? It cannot be denied that people in both countries see difficulties in the two nations' relationship. Changes in favorable feelings may derive in part from how we see our own prospects. As table 3–22 shows, perceptions fluctuate about which country will be the number one economic power in the world, with the Japanese less likely to see themselves in the role than they were seven years ago. Still, viewed over the long term, the suspicion that existed after the war seems largely to have disappeared. The cumulative weight of the polling evidence sees the two nations as committed allies.

TABLE 3–22
U.S. AND JAPANESE PREDICTIONS OF ECONOMIC PREDOMINANCE IN THE TWENTY-FIRST CENTURY, 1989–1994
(percent)

Question: In the next century, which country do you think will be the number one economic power in the world—the United States, Japan, or some other country?

	United States	Japan
Americans		
1989	47	38
1990	32	50
1991	30	52
1992	45	30
1993	43	35
1994	49	37
Japanese		
1989	40	45
1990	42	39
1991	29	53
1992	36	44
1993	31	44
1994	31	25

NOTE: Not all response categories are shown.
SOURCE: Surveys by CBS News/*New York Times* (U.S.) and Tokyo Broadcasting System (Japan), latest that of December 1994.

CHAPTER 4

Society and Social Values

Surveys are typically blunt instruments for exploring people's deepest feelings—their social ideals, religious beliefs, hopes and fears, assessments of current national performance, and expectations for the future. For fifteen years now, one of the authors of this book has been editing a magazine (first *Public Opinion*, then *The American Enterprise*) that has reviewed poll findings on these subjects on a continuing basis. For eighteen years, the other author has directed the largest extant library of public opinion information and has thus been required to monitor much of the huge flow of relevant survey findings. Even from these vantage points, we sometimes conclude that available data, for all their rich variety, fail to assess adequately the American public's most fundamental views and values bearing on their society.

If this is so in the case of American society—of which we are members and which we know by far the best—it becomes even more problematic when we seek to compare this society's views and values to those of others. We believe that it is essential to extend the reach of survey-based comparisons, and we are confident that this volume contributes to that end. This does not mean, though, that we should minimize the daunting obstacles—some inherent in the nature of polling itself—to broad-brush comparisons of two or more nations. How satisfied are Americans and Japanese with various key aspects of their lives and their societies' performances? How do they think about their work, their leisure time, their families, and the interaction between men and women? In the pages that follow, we assemble what we consider to be the most persuasive survey findings on these questions.

Recent U.S. and Japanese Social Experience

The late 1960s and much of the 1970s were a rocky time for the United States in many ways—from the bitter divisions surrounding the war in Vietnam, to the oil shocks and long lines at the gas pumps, to Watergate, to aggressive Soviet expansion in Asia and Africa. All manner of polling indicators documented a darkening public mood in the face of these developments. Many Americans were obviously angry at the actions and inaction of various leaders and felt that performance had fallen far short of what it should be. But we did not, of course, need polls to learn this. If all the polls did were to convey dissatisfaction with such developments, they would simply confirm the obvious. The mere fact of dissatisfaction was entirely unremarkable. The important question for survey research was: How deep was the dissatisfaction, and what consequences did it carry for national life? Reviewing survey findings in this area, one of us wrote in 1977 that much of the analysis by the press and by scholars alike failed to distinguish adequately where the public's response stood along a continuum on which "legitimacy crisis" occupied one end and "limited dissatisfaction with immediate performance" the other.[1]

At various intervals since the 1970s as well, Americans have faced real problems—such as that of the recession of the early 1990s. Every such experience with adversity and the intensely negative news coverage that accompanies it prompts polling that, predictably, finds public concern. The politically important dimension involves *intensity*. In considering this, imagine a scale on which every expression from satisfaction to dissatisfaction is designated between 0 and 100, according to its strength. Who would claim that a situation in which 70 percent of the public say they are dissatisfied, with an average intensity rating of 7, is comparable to one in which 70 percent are dissatisfied, with an average intensity rating of 87? The former would be the lightest of moods, easily swept away by a modest dose of good news. The latter would signify an anger capable of shaking the system's very foundation.

A variety of different indicators help us deal with the intensity dimension. For example, the degree of volatility in certain measures—in the context of what is actually going on in the society—can tell us much about how intense the feelings actually are. Looking to

---

1. Everett Ladd, "The Polls, the Question of Confidence," *Public Opinion Quarterly*, Winter 1976–1977, pp. 544–52.

U.S. experience in 1991–1992, the extreme volatility in the respons-es to the "Are you satisfied or dissatisfied?" questions is instructive. Many of these questions recorded near-record highs of satisfaction in the spring of 1991, followed by near-record lows in the spring of 1992. Sixty-six percent of those interviewed by Gallup in March 1991 said they were satisfied with "the way things were going in the Unit-ed States at this time," the highest figure that had been recorded in more than forty askings of the question over the preceding thirteen years. (Sixty-six percent also came down as "satisfied" in a March 1986 survey.) In striking contrast, just 14 percent of respondents to the June 1992 Gallup survey said they were satisfied—the second-low-est Gallup rating ever recorded. (The absolute lowest number, 12 percent satisfied, came in a survey taken in July 1979, the setting that prompted President Jimmy Carter's famous speech on American "malaise.")

The source of this rapid change is evident. The successful conclu-sion of the Persian Gulf War dominated the headlines in the spring of 1991, and this experience brought forth positive responses on dif-ferent types of questions tapping the public's mood. By the spring of 1992, however, stories of the recession were capturing the headlines. In addition, a presidential campaign was underway, replete with its inevitable faultfinding. In fact, the economic position of the United States did not change fundamentally between spring 1991 and spring 1992; and it is doubtful that Americans' thinking about their coun-try shifted in any major way either. The questions we have been cit-ing are general indicators of mood—and public moods fluctuate in every democratic nation. Little would be gained in this book by com-paring routine mood fluctuations in the United States and Japan.

The Media's Negative Message

In evaluating satisfaction in the United States and Japan, then, the key issue is often not the direction of assessments, positive or nega-tive, nearly so much as it is the *intensity* of such sentiments and, where change is envisioned, its extent or reach. We must also keep in mind, when reviewing data on the public's satisfaction/dissatisfaction with social performance, that a substantial part of the picture transcends individual nations' experiences and involves conditions present in most, if not all, industrial democracies. In 1993, for example, we reviewed survey findings from around the OECD world, showing in most of these countries high levels of expressed dissatisfaction with or pessimism about political and economic performance.[2] The reports then coming out of these prosperous, free, stable nations read as though each were gripped by some unique national malaise—but taken together, the reports told a remarkably similar story. The United States and Japan displayed high levels of professed public dissatisfaction—but so did Canada, France, Britain, Germany, Italy, and Spain.

Several contemporary phenomena help explain the high level of public dissatisfaction frequently expressed across the advanced industrial world. First, there appears to have been the discovery of a common insight in many of these countries, more or less at the same time, that money really doesn't buy happiness. These nations' economies are on the whole great success stories, but other aspects of their social development leave their citizens deeply concerned. Crime and family dislocation are, for example, far higher today in most of these countries than they were historically. Second, publics all across the industrial world seem not to know what to do about modern government. They see no alternative to its playing a large role, but they are dissatisfied with important aspects of its performance. Finally, it is striking to see how many of the indicators of public dissatisfaction began an upward climb at roughly the same time in many different countries—roughly at the onset of the television age.

Intense electronic, "global village" communication is a part of the advanced or "postindustrial" era. This communication process brings various problems—crime, terrorism, economic distress, and the like—into people's living rooms instantly and pervasively. Establishing the connection between this communication structure and the pessimism publics express about aspects of their societies' performances is difficult. Still, the data suggest a close connection—and assessments of national economies are a good case in point.

Every week in the United States since late 1985, ABC News and *Money* magazine have asked national samples a series of economic questions, including: "Would you describe the state of the nation's economy these days as excellent, good, not so good, or poor?" Subtracting the two negative assessments (not so good and poor) from the two positive ones, we get a score that in theory can run from +100 (everyone finding the economy in good-to-excellent shape) to –100. Examining this decade-long time series, we see that the weekly scores

---

2. Everett C. Ladd et al., "Why Are So Many People So Pessimistic in So Different Countries?" *The Public Perspective*, March/April 1993, p. 29.

track actual economic performance only very roughly. For example, while scores were far lower during the 1991 recession than during the 1988 boom, the average assessment was considerably lower during 1992—when the economy was actually improving—than during 1991, when it reached its recessionary low.

It is most striking that in the more than 400 askings of this question from December 1985 through December 1995, there is not a single instance when more people called the economy good-to-excellent than said it was not so good or poor. (It was even-steven on one occasion, April 1986, when 50 percent of the responses were positive and 50 percent were negative.) Thus, through a period of economic ups and downs but general prosperity, the index never got into the black. Nevertheless, when people were asked to assess their own economic position, they frequently gave highly positive accounts.

The pattern appears to be much the same in Japan. Surveys done by Chuo Chosa-Sha for Jiji Press regularly since 1981 have found professed dissatisfaction with the national economy similar to that in the United States. In the approximately 175 askings (July 1981 through December 1995) for a judgment on "general economic conditions" in Japan, more respondents came down on the "getting worse" side than on the "getting better" one, all but 20–25 times. Such negative readings of the economy seem almost an inevitable feature of life in the intense and pervasive, problem-stressing communications world experienced by the United States, Japan, and other advanced industrial nations.

Social Dissatisfaction Higher in Japan

Polls taken regularly in both countries show relatively high professed dissatisfaction—varying, of course, with current events and circumstances—with many aspects of economic performance and, as well, with national direction in general (table 4–1). But these data leave unanswered the question of *relative* dissatisfaction. Other data indicate, however, that discontents are somewhat greater in Japan than in the United States. In 1990, the *Wall Street Journal* and Nippon Research asked respondents in the two nations whether a list of statements involved matters more true of Americans or of the Japanese. Japanese respondents said "happy with their lives" was more true of people in the United States (28 percent) than in Japan (16 percent), though a strong plurality thought there was no general difference. In sharp contrast, Americans were much more inclined to say the state-

TABLE 4–1
DEGREE OF SATISFACTION WITH SOCIAL EXPERIENCE
IN THE UNITED STATES AND JAPAN, 1979–1994
(percent)

Question: In general, are you satisfied or dissatisfied with the way things are going in the United States at this time? In general, do you think Japan is headed in a good or a bad direction?

| | Americans | | Japanese | |
	Satisfied	Dissatisfied	Good	Bad
1979	26	69	36	29
1980	NA	NA	33	30
1981	17	78	34	31
1982	25	71	26	39
1983	35	59	32	34
1984	50	46	39	27
1985	51	46	39	26
1986	66	30	37	35
1987	45	49	43	29
1988	41	54	40	31
1989	45	50	49	25
1990	55	39	38	31
1991	37	60	40	36
1992	26	68	31	44
1993	34	63	30	45
1994	29	67	35	42

NOTE: NA = not available. Not all response categories are shown. For the U.S., from 1991 on, the last asking of this question each year is shown.
SOURCE: Surveys by the Gallup Organization (U.S.) and by the Prime Minister's Office (Japan), latest that of 1994.

ment was true of them (61 percent) than of the Japanese (21 percent). These answers in part reflect something we see in answers to many types of questions—American exuberance contrasted with Japanese reticence. The Japanese are typically more inclined to take a softer or middling response—here, more inclined to minimize national differences. At the same time, though, Americans typically give responses that suggest a more optimistic or satisfied judgment. This is true in matters involving their own personal life situations and true, too, in assessments of societies at large.

When asked in the early 1990s in polls taken for the World Values Study Group whether, taking all things together, "you would say you're happy or not happy with your own life," large majorities in both countries said they were happy; but the proportion making this claim in the United States (89 percent) was higher than that in Japan (77 percent). Two recent surveys done jointly in both countries provide further readings. One was taken by the *Wall Street Journal* and *Nihon Keizai Shimbun* in March 1995, the other by the Gallup Organization in April (see tables 4–2 and 4–3). More Americans than Japanese pronounced themselves satisfied in every one of the seventeen areas covered in the two surveys. This was true even in areas where, at least until very recently, Japan was thought to surpass the United States. Job security is an example (table 4–2). But in March 1995, 29 percent of Japanese pronounced themselves "not satisfied" with their job security, as against only 14 percent of Americans. Whereas 47 percent of respondents in the United States said they were just somewhat satisfied or not at all satisfied with the cost and coverage of their health plans, 78 percent of Japanese made this negative assessment.

Asking about twelve separate aspects of personal life, Gallup found in its April 1995 surveys that the "satisfaction gap" between Americans and Japanese was greatest in the areas of family income, housing, leisure time, and general standard of living. It was smallest in such areas as family life and community (table 4–3).

In June 1989, interviewers for the CBS News/*New York Times*/Tokyo Broadcasting System group asked respondents in the two countries whether they had "up to now" been able to satisfy most of their ambitions, or whether they had had to settle for less than they had hoped. Again, Americans were more positive. A solid majority (58 percent) said they had satisfied most of their ambitions (four in ten said they had not), while a narrow majority in Japan (53 percent) said they had had to settle for less than they had hoped. A Gallup survey taken in February 1990 for a private voluntary-action group, Junior Achievement, found young people in the United States professing much more optimism than their counterparts in Japan about actually being able to do the kind of work they wanted to do. Only 9 percent of young Japanese said they were certain that they would be able to find the work they most wanted, compared with 23 percent of young Americans. At the other end, 56 percent in Japan, as against just 28 percent in the United States, said it was only somewhat likely or unlikely that they would actually be able to gain the jobs they wanted.

TABLE 4–2
DEGREE OF SATISFACTION WITH ONE'S OWN POSITION
IN THE UNITED STATES AND JAPAN, 1995
(percent)

Question: Now I'm going to read you a list of items. For each item, please tell me how satisfied you are in this area—very satisfied, fairly satisfied, just somewhat satisfied, or not satisfied. First, are you very satisfied, fairly satisfied, just somewhat satisfied, or not satisfied with (read item) . . . ?

	Very Satisfied	Fairly Satisfied	Just Somewhat Satisfied	Not Satisfied
Americans				
Your job security	33	19	14	14
Your income, keeping up with the cost of living	15	27	23	33
Your ability to retire financially secure	17	21	23	35
The cost of housing	22	27	20	26
The cost and coverage of your health care	29	21	18	29
Japanese				
Your job security	6	9	42	29
Your income, keeping up with the cost of living	4	9	55	27
Your ability to retire financially secure	4	6	36	39
The cost of housing	10	10	32	27
The cost and coverage of your health care	6	9	45	33

NOTE: Not all response categories are shown.
SOURCE: Surveys by the *Wall Street Journal* (U.S.) and *Nihon Keizai Shimbun* (Japan), March 1995.

TABLE 4–3
PERCENTAGE OF AMERICANS AND JAPANESE VERY OR SOMEWHAT SATISFIED
WITH ASPECTS OF THEIR PERSONAL LIVES, 1995
(percent)

Question: How satisfied or dissatisfied are you with the way things are going in your personal life today?

	Americans	Japanese
Very/somewhat satisfied		
Personal life	83	60

Question: How satisfied are you with the following aspects of your life?

	Americans	Japanese
Very/somewhat satisfied		
Household income	71	44
Housing	90	63
Leisure time	80	56
Standard of living	75	51
Job/work	73	55
Food	95	79
Education	78	60
Durable goods	94	75
Health	86	69
Family life	91	74
Clothing	92	77
Community	86	77

SOURCE: Surveys by the Gallup Organization, April 1995.

Gender Relations

When asked by Roper Starch Worldwide (formerly the Roper Organization) in the United States and Dentsu, Inc. in Japan (in surveys conducted for Virginia Slims in 1989 and 1990) to assess the status of women, large majorities of women in both countries have since 1970 indicated that they see great economic improvements. This is true of salaries paid to women compared with men, and of the kinds of jobs and leadership positions open to them (table 4–4). (At the same time, women in both countries—and American women in particu-

TABLE 4–4
The Views of Japanese and American Women on Progress in Their Status, 1989 and 1990
(percent)

Question: Below is a list of things that have been widely discussed since the 1970s with regard to women in our society. Please circle one answer for each item whether you think since 1970 things for women have improved a lot, improved a little, gotten a little worse, gotten a lot worse, or haven't changed.

	American Women		Japanese Women	
	Have improved	Have gotten worse	Have improved	Have gotten worse
The kinds of jobs open to women	89	4	88	1
The salaries women are paid compared with what men are paid	86	4	81	1
Women's opportunities for leadership positions in business	79	6	73	2
The day-care options available to working mothers	72	14	74	3
Women's roles as homemakers	37	37	56	10
Women's roles as mothers	36	41	50	17
Women's opportunities for leadership positions in government	71	3	71	7
The kinds of marriages women have	34	45	59	10

NOTE: Roper Starch Worldwide repeated many of the questions in this survey in the United States in 1994. We show here the 1989–1990 data because surveys were done in both countries then. Not all response categories are shown.
SOURCE: Survey by Roper Starch Worldwide (U.S.), 1989, and Dentsu Inc. (Japan), 1990, for Virginia Slims/Philip Morris.

TABLE 4–5
AMERICAN AND JAPANESE WOMEN'S PERCEPTIONS
OF THEIR STATUS, 1989 AND 1990
(percent)

Question: Do you feel you stand an equal chance with the men you
work with in the following areas or not?

	American Women	Japanese Women
Salary	55	24
Responsibility	62	37
Promotion	50	18
Becoming an executive	41	15

NOTE: Roper Starch Worldwide repeated many of the questions in this survey
in the United States in 1994. We show here the 1989–1990 data because surveys were done in both countries then. Not all response categories are shown.
SOURCE: Survey by Roper Starch Worldwide (U.S.), 1989, and Dentsu Inc.
(Japan), 1990, for Virginia Slims/Philip Morris.

lar—are much less sanguine about whether progress has been made
in noneconomic areas, notably family life. We return to this subject
later in this chapter.) But if women in both countries see economic
progress, American women are far more positive about achieving
equal workplace opportunity. Thus 55 percent of American women
surveyed in 1989 said they thought they stood an equal chance with
men with whom they work in salary—a conviction expressed by only
24 percent of Japanese women (table 4–5).

Other surveys have regularly found that women's perceptions
bearing on workplace equality are more negative in Japan than in
the United States. In a question posed in October 1986 by Louis Harris and Associates and the *Asahi Shimbun,* 77 percent of the Japanese
surveyed said their country discriminates more against women, only
10 percent that the United States did. In the Roper/Dentsu poll
taken in 1989 and 1990, a majority of women in the United States (54
percent) said that the men with whom they worked really looked on
them as equals; only 31 percent of women in Japan thought this. In
September 1990, Japanese women were asked in a survey taken by
the Prime Minister's Office if men and women have achieved equality in the home, at work, in society at large, and in legal status.
Roughly equal numbers said that women had and had not achieved
legal equality (38 percent agreeing that they had, 37 percent dis-

agreeing); while 42 percent said that they had achieved equality in the home, and 39 percent dissented.

Results were lopsided against the view that equality had been achieved at work—with 52 percent of women saying it had not, only 19 percent that it had. The responses were much the same for society at large—55 percent saying that women had not achieved basic equality in the society, just 21 percent that they had. Those who said equality had not been achieved at work were then asked whether they thought it would come in the near future, someday but not soon, or never. Only 13 percent of these women expected it in the near future, 44 percent someday but not soon, and a strikingly high 37 percent that it would never come in Japan.

The idea that women and men are to be accorded full equality of status under the law, in the workplace and in other areas of social life, is a natural element of sociopolitical individualism. The point isn't that highly individualist societies—which the United States has historically been—have not at times failed to honor this commitment, because obviously they have. But a broadly individualist philosophy finds it hard to deny fundamental claims for gender equality. In contrast, traditional ascriptive class societies have posited differences in men's and women's roles across social life as part of a natural and immutable order. Not every traditional society has been patriarchal, but the vast preponderance have been, and feudal Japan was no exception.

In the fifty years since World War II, Japanese society has moved quite far from the male dominance that distinguished the country's gender relations historically. Clearly, however, it has not moved far enough, from the perspective of many Japanese women. Striking evidence of the progress made and the distance yet to go comes from a survey (the "Study of the Japanese National Character") begun in 1958 and conducted every five years since. In 1958 nearly two-thirds of Japanese women (64 percent) said they would rather be born a man when asked if they were to be born again and were able to choose their sex. By 1993 the proportion had declined sharply, but still stood at a high 29 percent (table 4–6). A Gallup survey taken in 1958 found that only 17 percent of women surveyed in the United States said that they would rather be born a man than a woman if they could be born again; 60 percent of Japanese women in this survey said they would.

Many traditional norms and assumptions bearing on gender roles and relationships remain at least partly in place in Japan. Put another way, gender relations have changed in both countries, but are vastly more in flux in Japan than in individualist America, where the

71

TABLE 4–6
WHETHER JAPANESE MEN AND WOMEN
WOULD RATHER BE MALE OR FEMALE, 1958–1993
(percent)

Question: If you were to be born again, would you want to be a man or a woman?

	Men Would Rather Be		Women Would Rather Be	
	Male	Female	Male	Female
1958	90	5	64	27
1963	88	7	55	36
1968	89	5	43	48
1973	89	5	42	51
1978	90	4	41	52
1983	90	5	39	56
1988	90	4	34	59
1993	88	3	29	65

NOTE: Not all response categories are shown.
SOURCE: The Study of Japanese National Character for the Institute of Statistical Mathematics, latest that of 1993.

patriarchal structure so common to traditionalist societies was never established.

Since this point can easily be misunderstood, we are at pains to restate it precisely. Our argument surely is not that American men or women would rest comfortably with certain values involving gender relations that prevailed earlier in the country's history. It was not until 1871 that women first got the vote anywhere in the United States (it was introduced in the territory of Wyoming), and not until 1921 that the nineteenth amendment establishing women's suffrage everywhere was enacted. This acknowledged, the United States should be compared with other societies at given times, rather than with itself over time. Gender relations in the United States in the early nineteenth century, for example, were vastly more egalitarian than those in European countries with ascriptive class traditions, and far more egalitarian than in Japan at that time. Numerous nineteenth-century Europeans visiting the United States described this American experience as remarkably egalitarian. James Bryce was one who saw women's rights more widely recognized in the United States than in Europe. This had resulted, Bryce argued, because

The root idea of democracy cannot stop at defining men as male human beings, any more than it could ultimately stop at defining them as white human beings. . . . Democracy is in America more respectful of the individual, less disposed to infringe his freedom or subject him to any sort of legal and family control, than it had shown itself in continental Europe, and this regard for the individual inured to the benefit of women."[3]

A half-century ago, sociologist Lee Coleman, applying a "lexicographic analysis," looked systematically at the huge volume of writing by foreign and domestic commentators on "the American way" in four historical periods: the years before the Civil War; from that war to World War I; the 1920s; and the 1930s, the latter two decades being those immediately preceding his study. Coleman found essentially the same values emphasized in each period—individualism, popular sovereignty, moral and social equality, limited government. "It will be observed," he concluded, that "when the lists for each of the four time periods were compared, no important difference between the traits mentioned by modern observers and those writing in the earlier periods of American history was discovered."[4] Given this historic emphasis on egalitarian values, recent changes in gender relations in the United States, while substantial, are necessarily far more limited than in Japan, a country with a strong feudal tradition.

Much more of the old order survives in that country. Thus, when NHK asked respondents in an October 1993 survey how much education they would like to see a son or daughter of theirs receive before entering the work force, 70 percent said they wanted the son to have a university education, while only 35 percent felt a daughter should. In contrast, 40 percent said she should have a senior high school, junior college, or vocational education—while only 9 percent felt he should. In another survey taken in the same month by the Prime Minister's Office, almost half (46 percent) agreed that a husband should have a higher educational background and social status than his wife. In some areas, inevitably, the more abrupt character of the value shift in Japan is producing deeper dissatisfaction—among those who

---

3. James Bryce, *The American Commonwealth*, volume 2, p. 808.
4. Lee Coleman, "What Is America? A Study of Alleged American Traits," *Social Forces*, volume 19, 1940–1941, pp. 492–99; the quotation is from p. 498.

believe the change is coming too slowly or incompletely, and among those uncomfortable with the amount of change already achieved.

The 1989–1990 Roper/Dentsu surveys asked women in both countries a battery of questions about "most men." The results would suggest that another way the dissatisfaction expresses itself is in more negative views about men in Japan. Japanese women were more likely than their American counterparts to believe that most men are basically selfish and self-centered (62 to 42 percent), interested in their work outside the home but not interested in things going on in the home (69 to 53 percent). Japanese women were less likely than American women to say that most men are kind, gentle, and thoughtful (37 to 51 percent).

Not only do women in Japan believe they face more discrimination in the workplace than do American women; they are also more likely to believe that a superior in the firm for which they work would not be supportive of them. A question posed in the 1989–1990 Roper/Dentsu surveys taken in the two countries uncovered an interesting expression of this greater sense of workplace vulnerability. Two-thirds of women in Japan, compared with only 26 percent in the United States, said they would be nervous about telling their boss they were expecting a baby!

We are not suggesting that a more vigorous assertion of individualist values is bound to produce general social amelioration. For example, we see in the data reported in table 4–4 (above) that while large majorities of American women believe that contemporary change has improved the position of most women in the workplace, they have very different, far more negative assessments about the implications for family life. Only 34 percent said that the changes of the past two decades have improved things in terms of "the kinds of marriages women have," while 45 percent said things have gotten worse (again, see table 4–4).

In contrast, in Japan, where less egalitarian norms apply, women are markedly more inclined to report improved conditions. For example, 59 percent say things have improved in terms of the kinds of marriages women have, while only 10 percent say they have gotten worse. Being "more advanced" hardly guarantees greater satisfaction in every instance. One hundred fifty years ago, in his description of the rush to modernity, which represents an ever more substantial assertion of social and political individualism, Tocqueville was at pains to stress what he saw as negative features of the emergent order, along with positive aspects. He thought that more individual-

74

istic and egalitarian social relations would come almost inevitably; he did not believe that this guaranteed happiness. Wherever a more complete assertion of the new order encounters problems, Americans are likely to manifest relatively high levels of discontent, because they are likely to be further along in experiencing them.

In Japan as in the United States, women have entered the paid labor force in large numbers. In 1992, the labor force participation rate for Japanese women was 51 percent, compared with 58 percent for American women. The labor force participation rate for young (20–24–year-old) women in Japan was actually higher (76 percent) than for their American counterparts (71 percent). For all women in the peak employment years (ages 25–54), the proportion in the labor force in 1990 was higher in the United States (74 percent) than in Japan (65 percent), but the basic story is that it is high in both countries. Asked in 1994 as part of the International Social Survey Programme (ISSP) whether they agreed or disagreed that "both the husband and the wife should contribute to the household income," 54 percent of Japanese replied in the affirmative, almost exactly the same percentage as of Americans (57 percent). And indeed, among Japanese women, the proportion strongly agreeing that as a general rule both spouses should bring in paychecks was 14 percentage points higher than that among American women, indicating strong agreement (table 4–7).

This noted, Japanese women remain more tolerant than American women of norms and practices stressing women's primary responsibilities in the home and for the family. Thus, 47 percent of Japanese women, as against just 19 percent of American women, strongly agreed that "being a housewife is just as fulfilling as working for pay." Similarly, women in Japan are more inclined than American women to resist the idea of women's participating full-time in the labor force when they have school-age children (tables 4–7 and 4-8).

The 1994 ISSP survey found American women reporting what seems to be fairly close to an even division on the question of which spouse does the most by way of household chores (table 4–9). When it comes to laundry, they say the woman mostly does it, while on small repairs around the house, the man usually does. But on many things, including caring for sick family members and shopping for groceries, women in the United States are about as likely to say that it is an equal responsibility of both the man and the woman as to say it usually falls to them. To be sure, outside the traditional male domain, few American women or men report a situation where a

75

TABLE 4–7
THE VIEWS OF AMERICANS AND JAPANESE ON MARRIAGE, FAMILY, AND WORK, 1994
(percent)

Statement: The main advantage of marriage is that it gives financial security

	Strongly Agree	Agree
All Americans	3	14
All Japanese	20	21
American women	3	13
Japanese women	21	21

Statement: Watching children grow up is life's greatest joy

	Strongly Agree	Agree
All Americans	35	46
All Japanese	60	24
American women	37	45
Japanese women	63	23

Statement: People who have never had children lead empty lives

	Strongly Agree	Agree
All Americans	3	15
All Japanese	43	18
American women	3	14
Japanese women	42	17

Statement: When there are children in the family, parents should stay together even if they don't get along

	Strongly Agree	Agree
All Americans	3	12
All Japanese	37	20
American women	2	10
Japanese women	34	17

Statement: One parent can bring up a child as well as two parents together

	Strongly Agree	Agree
All Americans	9	27
All Japanese	38	19
American women	11	32
Japanese women	38	19

Statement: Both the husband and the wife should contribute to the household income

	Strongly Agree	Agree
All Americans	20	37
All Japanese	35	19
American women	22	36
Japanese women	36	20

Statement: It is not good if the man stays at home and cares for the children and the woman goes out to work

	Strongly Agree	Agree
All Americans	7	16
All Japanese	26	12
American women	7	15
Japanese women	26	11

TABLE 4–7 (continued)

Statement: Being a housewife is just as fulfilling as working for pay

All Americans	17	38
All Japanese	44	20
American women	19	37
Japanese women	47	20

Statement: What women really want is a home and children

All Americans	7	25
All Japanese	33	15
American women	7	25
Japanese women	32	16

Statement: A preschool child is likely to suffer if his or her mother works

All Americans	9	32
All Japanese	15	22
American women	9	27
Japanese women	15	23

Statement: A man's job is to earn money, a woman's job is to look after the home and family

All Americans	5	16
All Japanese	20	19
American women	5	12
Japanese women	19	17

Statement: Working women should receive paid maternity leave when they have a baby

All Americans	28	46
All Japanese	86	8
American women	32	46
Japanese women	87	8

Statement: Families should receive financial benefits for child care when both parents work

All Americans	15	30
All Japanese	48	19
American women	18	31
Japanese women	46	21

NOTE: Not all response categories are shown.

SOURCE: Surveys by National Opinion Research Center (U.S.), February–May 1994, and International Social Survey Programme (ISSP) (Japan), January 15–23, 1994.

TABLE 4–8
AMERICAN AND JAPANESE VIEWS ON WORKING MOTHERS, 1993
(percent)

Question: Do you think that women should work outside the home full-time, part-time, or not at all under these circumstances:

	Americans			Japanese		
	Full-time	Part-time	Not at all	Full-time	Part-time	Not at all
After marrying and before there are children	75	12	2	66	20	7
When there is a child under school age	10	31	49	10	23	57
After the youngest child starts school	34	48	8	16	51	24
After the children leave home	70	14	2	48	33	8

NOTE: Not all response categories are shown.
SOURCE: Surveys by the International Social Survey Programme (ISSP), 1993.

man does the bulk of the household work. But roughly equal division is now commonly reported.

Not so in Japan, where among the items covered in the 1994 ISSP survey, Japanese women and men alike report that household tasks fall almost exclusively to the woman, except in the case of household repairs. Even there, a quarter of Japanese women say they always or usually handle the task (table 4–9). In the 1989–1990 Roper/Dentsu surveys, respondents were asked about things that make them feel resentful. Nearly two-thirds of Japanese women (65 percent) compared with just a third (35 percent) of U.S. women said they felt resentful often or from time to time about "the amount of time I spend [on] family responsibilities."

It is doubtful that we have any real sense of whether Americans and Japanese differ in terms of how "child-centered" they are. Kids are obviously the objects of great love and pride to many people in both countries, although parents may express such feelings differently, especially as filtered through the vocabulary of survey research

TABLE 4–9
DIVISION OF HOUSEHOLD CHORES IN THE UNITED STATES AND JAPAN, 1994
(percent)

Question: In your household who does the following things...?

	Always/ Usually the Woman	About Equal or Both	Always/ Usually the Man
Does the laundry			
All Americans	69	25	4
All Japanese	93	4	1
American women	71	25	3
Japanese women	93	4	1
Makes small repairs around the house			
All Americans	5	21	17
All Japanese	18	10	68
American women	9	25	62
Japanese women	24	11	60
Cares for sick family members			
All Americans	48	47	2
All Japanese	74	18	1
American women	54	43	1
Japanese women	81	12	1
Shops for groceries			
All Americans	49	44	7
All Japanese	77	18	a
American women	51	43	5
Japanese women	79	18	a
Decides what to have for dinner			
All Americans	55	39	6
All Japanese	90	5	1
American women	61	36	3
Japanese women	93	4	1

NOTE: Not all response categories are shown.
a. Less than 1 percent.
SOURCE: Surveys by National Opinion Research Center (U.S.), February–May 1994, and International Social Survey Programme (ISSP) (Japan), January 15–23, 1994.

questions. Nonetheless, surveys do show Japanese women and men alike saying much more commonly than Americans that families without children lead empty lives (see, again, table 4–7). Relatedly, Japanese are much more of the view that when there are children in the family, parents should stay together even "if they don't get along." In individualist America, such an argument finds markedly less agreement (table 4–7). As we noted in chapter 2, divorce rates are only half as high in Japan as in the United States. Perhaps because they have much less experience than Americans of single-parent households, both Japanese women and men are much more inclined than Americans to say that one parent can bring up a child as well as two parents together (table 4–7).

In a survey taken in December 1994 for the *Asahi Shimbun*, Japanese respondents were asked which among four different types of families they considered the ideal (table 4–10). The responses will strike many Americans as "male chauvinist." Nearly one in five endorsed as ideal a family situation where the "wife is obedient and dedicated to her husband." No survey research organization would even consider offering such a response alternative in the United States. At the other end of the continuum, only about one in five in Japan endorsed as ideal an alternative that was intended to reflect essential equality in the husband's and wife's family roles and responsibilities.

While noting these substantial differences between Americans and Japanese on questions involving gender relations and the family, we must emphasize that public thinking on these issues is evolving in both countries and, not surprisingly, is changing much more rapidly in Japan than in the United States. At intervals since 1974, Roper Starch Worldwide has asked Americans which of six contrasting family relationships they find the most satisfying. As table 4–11 shows, the proportion endorsing what the question describes as a "traditional" marriage in which the husband is the principal wage earner and the wife runs the house and takes care of the kids has declined over the past two decades but still is described as best by roughly four in ten of women and men alike. In Japan, surveys taken for the Prime Minister's Office have similarly asked at regular intervals over the past two decades whether respondents accept traditional Japanese roles for men and women or reject them. As table 4–11 indicates, support for this aspect of the old order has dropped precipitously. Whereas just 10 percent of Japanese women said they did not accept traditional gender roles in the 1972 survey, by 1984, half of them did. Similarly, the proportion of Japanese saying they

TABLE 4–10
SUPPORT FOR TRADITIONAL FAMILY STRUCTURE IN JAPAN, 1994
(percent)

Question: Which of the following four types of families do you think is ideal?

Type of Household	Percent Approve
Patriarchal household in which the wife is obedient and dedicated to her husband	17
Husband provides income for the family while the wife takes care of the house and children	20
Wife is responsible for the house and children, although the husband also shows concern for his family	41
Husband and wife each are deeply involved in their own jobs and activities	19

Question: Which type of man do you tend to approve of—a man who gives priority to his family life or to his work?

Type of Man	Percent Approve
Gives priority to his family life	44
Gives priority to his work	34
Difficult to say	22

Question: Which type of woman do you tend to approve of—a woman who gives priority to her family life or to her work?

Type of Woman	Percent Approve
Gives priority to her family life	77
Gives priority to her work	8
Difficult to say	15

NOTE: Percentages may not add to 100 because of rounding.
SOURCE: Survey by the *Asahi Shimbun*, December 1994.

thought women should quit work and "look after their house and family" after marriage dropped by half (from 35 percent to 18 percent) between 1973 and 1993 (table 4–12).

The greater measure of individualism and egalitarianism evident in the findings on gender relations can also be seen in the values stressed in child rearing. In its spring 1994 General Social Survey, the

TABLE 4–11
SUPPORT FOR TRADITIONAL MARRIAGE
IN THE UNITED STATES AND JAPAN, 1972–1995
(percent)

Question: In today's society there are many different lifestyles and some that are acceptable today that weren't in the past. Regardless of what you may have done or plan to do with your life, and thinking just of what would give you personally the most satisfying and interesting life, which one of these different ways of life do you think would be the best way of life?

	Traditional Marriage with the Husband Assuming the Responsibility for Providing for the Family and the Wife Running the House and Taking Care of the Children	A Marriage Where the Husband and Wife Share Responsibilities More— Both Work, Both Share Homemaking and Child Responsibilities
American women		
1974	50	46
1980	42	52
1985	37	57
1989	38	53
1994	37	50
American men		
1974	48	44
1980	42	49
1985	43	50
1989	39	50
1994	36	47

Question: Do you accept or reject traditional Japanese roles for men and women?

	Accept Traditional Roles	Reject Traditional Roles
Japanese women		
1972	83	10
1979	70	23
1984	49	50
1989	51	49

TABLE 4–11 (continued)

	Accept Traditional Roles	Reject Traditional Roles
Japanese men		
1972	84	9
1979	76	17
1984	63	37
1989	59	41

NOTE: Not all response categories are shown.
SOURCES: For top panel, surveys by Roper Starch Worldwide for Virginia Slims/Philip Morris, latest that of 1994. For bottom panel, surveys by the Prime Minister's Office.

National Opinion Research Center asked Americans which among a list of things they would choose as the most important for a child to learn to prepare him or her for life. One response—"to think for himself or herself"—was chosen by three times the proportion of respondents as that selecting any other (table 4–13). Just 1 percent picked "to be well liked." In contrast, when the *Yomiuri Shimbun* asked a similar question to Japanese respondents, "not bothersome to others" was easily the top vote-getter (table 4–13).

Workplace Satisfactions and Dissatisfactions

The greater degree of dissatisfaction shown by Japanese, compared with Americans, in other areas of social life is evident with reference to work life. The World Values Survey found many respondents in both countries expressing general satisfaction with their jobs, but 65 percent of Japanese, as compared with 79 percent of Americans, reported high satisfaction—defined here as rating oneself between 7 and 10 on a 10-point dissatisfied-to-satisfied continuum. In the surveys done by CBS/NYT/TBS in June 1989, 88 percent of employed people surveyed in the United States called their work interesting, compared with only 58 percent of those in Japan. Only a small number of Japanese respondents said they did not have an opinion on this question—although, as we have pointed out, such nonresponse is often considerably higher in Japan than in the United States. Just 12 percent of Americans said their work was "not interesting," but 37 percent of Japanese said this of their jobs.

Another set of questions posed in July 1985 and again in June 1989 by the CBS/NYT/TBS polls show this same higher incidence of work-

TABLE 4–12
CHANGE IN ATTITUDES TOWARD WORK AND FAMILY IN JAPAN, 1973–1993
(percent)

Question: How do you feel about women who continue to work after they are married?

	Women Should Quit Work and Look after Their House and Family after They Are Married	Women Should Continue Working until They Have a Baby	If Circumstances Permit, Women Should Continue Working after They Have a Baby
1973	35	42	20
1978	30	41	27
1983	29	40	29
1988	24	39	33
1993	18	41	37

NOTE: Not all response categories are shown.
SOURCE: Surveys by NHK, latest that of May 1993.

related dissatisfactions in Japan. Many Americans believe that the Japanese, more collectively inclined, are consequently more "loyal" to the organizations they work for than are the more individualist Americans. The survey responses suggest otherwise—perhaps because Japanese in general feel greater distance or estrangement from many central social institutions, corporations among them—a subject discussed at some length in chapter 5. The question posed in the two surveys asked respondents which of two positions was closer to their own, that "employees should work primarily for their own satisfaction and success" or that "employees should work primarily for the success of the company or organization" employing them. In the 1985 asking, by 51 to 40 percent, the Japanese said "work for one's own personal satisfaction." In contrast, by 49 to 32 percent, Americans said they work for the company's success. Four years later, the split was even sharper. By 78 to 20 percent, Japanese said working for one's own success came closer to their view, while by 48 to 33 percent Americans said working for the company's well-being was more important.

Leisure and the Work Ethic

Evidence from both countries suggests that as we have become more

84

TABLE 4–13
AMERICAN AND JAPANESE PARENTS' HIGHEST HOPES
FOR THEIR CHILDREN, 1994
(percent)

Question: Which thing . . . would you pick as the most important for a child to learn to prepare him or her for life?

Americans	
To think for himself or herself	54
To obey	18
To work hard	15
To help others when they need	13
To be well-liked or popular	1

Question: What type of people do you want your children to become, did you want them to become, or would you want them to become?

Japanese	
Not bothersome to others	43
Have abundant knowledge	20
Likable people	18
Useful to society	16
People of high social status	1

NOTE: Percentages may not add to 100 because of rounding.
SOURCE: For top panel, survey by the National Opinion Research Center, February–May 1994. For bottom panel, survey by the *Yomiuri Shimbun*, December 1994.

affluent and as labor-saving technology has proliferated, leisure time and leisure pursuits have become more important. Recently, Japan changed its regular work week from six days to five—a move that the United States made some fifty-five years earlier.[5] In 1973, NHK surveyed the Japanese public and asked respondents to locate their own views on the relationship between work and free time among five possible responses—ranging from the equivalent of "leisure is everything to me" to "I live for my work." NHK repeated this same question fifteen years later. As table 4–14 shows, the two most work-centered responses dropped by a net of 13 percentage points over this

5. The Fair Labor Standards Act of 1938 included a provision for a forty-hour work week. This provision of the act was implemented in 1940.

TABLE 4–14
JAPANESE VIEWS ON WORK AND LEISURE, 1973 AND 1988
(percent)

Question: The following list contains various opinions on the relationship between work and free time. Which comes closest to your
opinion?

	1973	1988
In my leisure activities, as compared to my work, I find something to live for	4	6
I do my work quickly and then enjoy my free time as much as possible	28	28
I devote about the same amount of my effort to my work and my free time	21	32
Although I enjoy free time sometimes, I devote more of my efforts to work	36	26
I live for my work, and devote all my energies to it	8	5

NOTE: Not all response categories are shown.
SOURCE: Surveys by NHK, latest that of June 1988.

span. Those choosing the response that "although I enjoy free time
sometimes, I devote more of my efforts to work" dropped from 36
percent in 1973 to 26 percent in 1988.

Another question asked by the Prime Minister's Office in Japan sup-
ports this notion of a shift in thinking about work and leisure, toward
greater emphasis on the latter. When asked in 1970 to which they
would like to give priority, preparing for the future by saving and
investment or living a full life everyday, nearly twice as many respondents (54 percent) said they would prepare for the future by saving
and investment than (28 percent) said they would live life to the full
each day. By 1993, the proportions had reversed rather sharply; 49 percent now said they would give priority to living life fully, only 37 percent to saving for the future (table 4–15). A companion question
posed by surveys sponsored by the Prime Minister's Office has found
an increase in what sociologist Ronald Inglehart[6] calls postmaterialist

6. Ronald Inglehart, *The Silent Revolution: Changing Values and Political Styles among
Western Publics* (Princeton, New Jersey: Princeton University Press, 1977); and Inglehart, *Culture Shift in Advanced Industrial Society* (Princeton, New Jersey: Princeton University Press, 1990).

TABLE 4–15
JAPANESE PRIORITIES FOR THE FUTURE, 1970–1993
(percent)

Question: Looking ahead, would you like: to be investing and saving money for the future, or just living happily day by day?

	Living Happily Day by Day	Investing and Saving Money
1970	28	54
1971	28	51
1972	33	44
1973	36	48
1974	39	43
1975	40	40
1976	42	41
1977	39	43
1978	39	42
1979	42	40
1980	39	45
1981	39	46
1982	41	44
1983	41	43
1984	40	46
1985	41	43
1986	43	40
1987	45	41
1988	45	39
1989	46	38
1990	47	38
1991	48	38
1992	51	34
1993	49	37

NOTE: Not all response categories are shown.
SOURCE: Surveys by the Prime Minister's Office, latest that of 1993.

values. Choosing the response "as I become fairly rich in a material sense, I will attach greater importance to spiritual riches" has increased markedly over the past two decades, while "I attach greater importance to material riches in life" has declined (table 4–16).

Other survey work done by NHK in March 1993 and January 1994

TABLE 4–16
JAPANESE VIEWS ON SPIRITUAL AND MATERIAL RICHES, 1972–1993
(percent)

Question: Which of these perspectives is closer to your view? As I become fairly rich in a material sense, I will attach greater importance to spiritual riches and to a full life; or I will attach greater importance to material riches in life.

	Spiritual Riches	Material Riches
1972	37	40
1973	35	40
1974	37	42
1975	39	41
1976	41	41
1977	40	41
1978	40	40
1979	41	40
1980	42	40
1981	44	40
1982	45	39
1983	46	38
1984	47	37
1985	50	37
1986	49	33
1987	50	33
1988	50	34
1989	49	32
1990	53	32
1991	52	31
1992	57	27
1993	57	29

NOTE: Not all response categories are shown.
SOURCE: Surveys by the Prime Minister's Office, latest that of 1993.

shows a similar evolution in Japanese thinking. Half of all respondents in each survey (50 percent in 1993, 49 percent in 1994) said that increasing their free time, even if it meant decreasing their income, was the preference closest to their view, as opposed to increasing their income even if it meant decreasing their leisure time (the response of

45 percent in 1993 and 44 percent the following year).

Polls taken in the United States over the past quarter-century have shown considerable concern that the American work ethic—so intimately linked to the country's economic success historically—may somehow be in decline. Though from a different (higher) base than Japan's, the United States has also experienced great increases in material abundance over the past half-century and, again like Japan, has displayed some shift toward leisure-emphasizing and "postmaterialist" attitudes.[7]

Still, any suggestion that Americans are losing their position as a people who give relatively high value to work is contradicted by survey findings (as well as by much behavioral data). In spring 1995, for example, Gallup asked respondents in a number of different countries, including the United States and Japan, how important various activities are in their lives. Many more Americans than Japanese described work as very important to them. While some of this large difference may be attributable to the general disposition we have noted, in which Japanese respondents prefer more moderate responses, it is striking that 18 percent of young Japanese said work is not important at all to them, the position of just 8 percent of young Americans (table 4–17).

Of course, when people care deeply about something, as both the Japanese and Americans do about the work ethic, they are likely to worry about it and see it deteriorating. In February 1989, CBS/NYT/TBS pollsters asked their respondents whether the generation born after World War II worked as hard as its parents did. Majorities in both countries (62 percent in the United States and 57 percent in Japan) said they did not. Majorities of those under age forty-five in both countries took this position. Huge majorities in both countries in the World Values Survey said they felt that a decrease in the importance of work would be a bad thing if it happened.

Findings from the World Values Survey similarly show Americans ranking highly, compared with the Japanese and with many other

---

7. Actually, we consider this commonly used term for the shift to be somewhat misleading. With greater affluence comes greater emphasis on values further along the continuum from subsistence needs. Quite naturally, poorer societies give less emphasis to cleaning up the environment than do richer ones. In the United States, the vast preponderance of Americans are more supportive of environmental causes now than they were three decades or more ago. We think this is less the replacing of materialism with postmaterialism than it is a natural evolution of material goals and expectations. We have discussed these findings at length in a recent report, *Attitudes toward the Environment: Twenty-Five Years after Earth Day* (Washington, D.C.: AEI Press, 1995).

TABLE 4–17

THE IMPORTANCE OF WORK TO AMERICANS AND JAPANESE, 1995
(percent)

Question: Please say, for each of the following, how important it is in your life . . . Work?

	Very Important	Quite Important	Not Important
All Americans	62	24	13
All Japanese	39	42	15
Young Americans (18–29 years)	68	24	8
Young Japanese (18–29 years)	24	51	18

NOTE: Not all response categories are shown.
SOURCE: Surveys by the Gallup Organization, April 1995.

peoples, on merit and achievement values relating to one's job. The survey presented respondents with a list of job-related considerations and asked them which they thought were important. As table 4–18 indicates, many more Japanese chose leisure-time benefits and interpersonal dimensions of the job, whereas Americans put more emphasis on such elements as getting ahead through promotions and "achieving something." The responses shown in table 4–18 are congruent with our general argument—that although popular sentiment is evolving in the same general direction in both countries, American attitudes continue to reflect a more pervasive individualism.

Given their emphasis on interpersonal relations at work and also on consensus, it will be difficult for the Japanese to move toward a system based on individual ability rather than seniority. A question from the World Values Survey asks respondents in both countries to think about a situation in which two secretaries are of the same age and doing practically the same job. One earns more ($50 a week) because she is quicker, more efficient, and more reliable on the job. Eighty percent of those surveyed in the United States thought this was fair, just 15 percent unfair. A much smaller percentage in Japan said it was fair (48 percent), and a third said it was not. Perhaps in part because the Japanese believe the American workplace is more competitive than their own, three-quarters of the Japanese in a 1991 CBS/NYT/TBS

TABLE 4–18
THE IMPORTANCE OF VARIOUS JOB ASPECTS TO AMERICANS AND JAPANESE, 1990–1993
(percent)

Question: Here are some aspects of a job that people say are important. Please look at them and tell me which ones you personally think are important in a job.

	Americans	Japanese
Generous holidays	31	52
Meets my abilities	58	71
Meeting people	38	48
No pressure	33	42
Pleasant people	75	78
Useful to society	42	42
Good hours	56	55
Good pay	85	78
Responsible job	57	48
Job security	73	58
Job respected	43	26
Use initiative	52	34
Achieve something	72	48
Job interesting	69	36
Promotions	58	23

NOTE: Not all response categories are shown.
SOURCE: World Values Survey, 1990–1993.

survey said working for a U.S. employer would bother them; only 20 percent said they would be willing to work for one. By contrast, when the pollsters asked Americans the same question, majorities said they would be willing to work for a Japanese company.

The Place of Religion

Political sociologist Seymour Martin Lipset has written insightfully on the theme that the United States and Japan are two "exceptional" nations. The concept of "exceptionalism," often applied to assessments of America's sociopolitical development, is similarly applicable, Lipset believes, to Japan—though the respective natures of Japanese and American exceptionalism are different indeed.[8] The word *exceptional* carries two quite different meanings in ordinary usage: one connotes being exceptionally good or unusually meritorious; the other, more literally, being a great exception—very different from others to which the subject might be compared. The term is understood here with the latter meaning.

Exceptionalism in America and Japan is nowhere better illustrated than in religion. Researchers making cross-cultural comparisons are properly cautioned about the pitfalls in too-sweeping generalizations. Here, though, while it is indeed sweeping, we think it is valid to say of the United States that it is exceptionally religious, and of Japan that it is exceptionally irreligious. This is not in any way to deny the large spiritual, nonmaterialist component of Japanese life, something evident now as historically. It is to say that many Japanese themselves do not understand their spiritual life in religious terms, and that the proportion calling themselves religious is smaller now than it was, even a quarter-century ago.

Few who study the American religious experience would question the first half of this generalization. Many have noted that religiously, the United States does not behave as it "should," in view of its economic, technological, scientific, "postindustrial" development. Walter Dean Burnham, a political scientist at the University of Texas, has observed that "the proposition suggests itself that the higher the level of development in a given society [meaning here, the closer it is to advanced industrialism], the smaller will be the fraction of its population for whom religious beliefs are of great importance."[9] Burnham tested this proposition by locating a large number of countries on two measures: the extent of their economic development, and the extent to which their citizens see religious beliefs as important in their lives. "Two things are immediately visible on inspection," Burnham wrote. "First, the overall relationship is not only positive, it is nearly linear and extremely strong." Burnham found that in general the more developed the country, the lower the importance citizens at large typically attached to religion. But the United States did

---

8. Seymour Martin Lipset, "American Exceptionalism—Japanese Uniqueness," in *American Exceptionalism: A Double-edged Sword* (New York: W.W. Norton, 1996).
9. Walter Dean Burnham, "The 1980 Earthquake: Realignment, Reaction, or What?" in Thomas Ferguson and Joel Rogers, eds., *The Hidden Election: Politics and Economics in the 1980 Presidential Campaign* (New York: Pantheon Books, 1981), p. 132.

not fit the pattern. It is highly developed and very religious.

George Gallup, Jr., a leading figure in survey research who has examined American religious belief and practice closely in his polls, has concluded that

> Americans' concerns about society, democracy and the future are deeply rooted in their beliefs about God. While most survey respondents hold staunchly to the view that one can be a good and ethical person without believing in God, a solid majority (61 percent) say that a democracy cannot survive without a widespread belief in God or a Supreme Being. Further evidence of the power of the religious dynamic in U.S. society is seen in the fact that the importance one places on religion, and the intensity of one's faith, often has more to do with attitudes and behavior than such background characteristics as age, level of education, and political affiliation.[10]

Gallup notes further that America's status as an unusually religious nation is cemented by behavior, not just opinion survey findings. "Nearly 500,000 churches, temples and mosques, of all shapes and sizes, dot the landscape. There are no fewer than 2,000 denominations, not to mention countless independent churches and faith communities."[11] What's more, the data show no weakening in such religious practice. "Clearly the United States is a 'churched' nation," Gallup continues; "in fact, the last fifty years have been the most churched half-century in the nation's history, judging from census and other data reported by Roger Finke and Rodney Stark."[12]

Gallup drew on his extensive research on Americans' religious beliefs. His surveys have found virtually all Americans saying they believe in God or in a universal spirit. Nine in ten attest to a belief in heaven, eight in ten that God performs miracles today. Seven in ten among American adults belong to a church or a synagogue, and six in ten say that religion is "very important" in their lives.

Japan is dramatically different. The World Values Survey found just over a third of Japanese respondents saying they believe in God (table 4–19), and only a small fraction of this group said they believe in a personal God (table 4–20). Whereas 80 percent of Americans

---

10. George Gallup, Jr., "Religion in America: Will the Vitality of Churches Be the Surprise of the Next Century?" *The Public Perspective*, October–November 1995, pp. 1–8.
11. Ibid., p. 1.
12. See Roger Finke and Rodney Stark, *The Churching of America* (New Brunswick, N.J.: Rutgers University Press, 1992).

TABLE 4–19
AMERICAN AND JAPANESE RELIGIOUS BELIEF, 1990–1993
(percent)

Question: Which, if any, of the following do you believe in?

	Americans	Japanese
God	93	37
Life after death	70	30
A soul	88	50
The Devil	65	10
Hell	66	17
Heaven	82	23
Sin	86	13
Resurrection of the dead	64	6
Reincarnation	21	29

SOURCE: World Values Survey, 1990–1993.

surveyed had been brought up religiously at home, only 22 percent of the Japanese surveyed said they had had religious upbringing (table 4–21). And, whereas 58 percent of Americans subscribe to the statement that "life is meaningful only because God exists," just 13 percent of Japanese agreed with it.

Other work done by Japanese survey organizations yields a similar picture. Thus a 1994 survey by the *Yomiuri Shimbun* found only 36 percent of respondents saying they believed one's "soul exists even after death" (table 4–22). And in another survey done by NHK in 1994, just 35 percent said they believed in God, 13 percent in "the afterworld or heaven," while 16 percent said they believe in the power of amulets or charms, and 24 percent in "nothing that relates to religion" (table 4–22). What's more, surveys taken by the *Yomiuri Shimbun* on five occasions from 1979 through 1995 show a steadily decreasing proportion of the Japanese indicating they believe that "religion is necessary for a happy life" or professing any form of religious affiliation (table 4–23).

The polls' depiction of Japanese irreligion is supported by the assessments of observers with long experience in the country. For example, Ian Buruma, a Dutch-born journalist and author, has written insightfully on postwar Japan, drawing on his long experience

13. Ian Buruma, *The Wages of Guilt: Memories of War in Germany and Japan* (New York: Penguin Books, 1995).

TABLE 4–20
AMERICAN AND JAPANESE BELIEF IN A HIGHER BEING, 1990–1993
(percent)

Question: Which . . . statement . . . comes closest to your beliefs?

	Americans	Japanese
There is a personal God	67	4
There is some sort of spirit or life force	23	29
I don't really know what to think	6	39
I don't really think there is any sort of spirit, God, or life force	2	8
Not answered	2	21

SOURCE: World Values Survey, 1990–1993.

there in the 1970s and 1980s.[13] Buruma tells the story of the protests prompted by the remarks of Nagasaki Mayor Motoshima Hitoshi at the time of the death of the Emperor Hirohito in 1989.

> The emperor was dying very, very slowly, losing large quantities of blood every day. He was dying of cancer. But in the climate of "self-restraint" this was never mentioned in the Japanese press. The atmosphere in Japan, in the dying days of the Showa era, was muted. . . . On December 7, a Communist party representative in the Nagasaki city assembly asked [the mayor] a straightforward question: What about the emperor's war guilt?
>
> Motoshima answered: "Forty-three years have passed since the end of the war, and I think we have had enough chance to reflect on the nature of that war. From reading various accounts from abroad and having been a soldier myself, involved in military education, I do believe that the emperor bore responsibility for the war."[14]

A firestorm of public reaction ensued, and in the midst of it, one extremist protester shot the mayor in the back. He barely survived the wound.

Motoshima was a Christian. He believed, Buruma writes, that this gave him a very different perspective on life from that of most other Japanese.

14. Ibid., p. 249.

TABLE 4–21
AMERICAN AND JAPANESE VIEWS ON RELIGION AND
THE MEANING OF LIFE, 1990–1993
(percent)

Question: Do you agree or disagree [with the following state-
ments] . . . ? [% agree]

	Americans	Japanese
Life is meaningful only because God exists.	58	13
The meaning of life is that you try to get the best out of it.	82	72
Death is inevitable, it is pointless to worry about it.	80	39
Death has a meaning only if you believe in God.	46	7
If you have lived your life, death is a natural resting point.	79	43
In my opinion, sorrow and suffering only have meaning if you believe in God.	33	11

Question: Which [statement] comes closest to your own point of
view . . . ? [% agree]

	Americans	Japanese
There are absolutely clear guidelines about what is good and evil. These always apply to everyone, whatever the circumstances.	49	13
There can never be absolutely clear guidelines about what is good and evil. . . . [It] depends entirely upon the circumstances at the time.	44	66

Question: Were you brought up religiously at home? [% yes]	80	22

Question: [W]hether you go to church or not, would you say you are . . . a religious person? [% yes]	82	21

SOURCE: World Values Survey, 1990–1993.

TABLE 4–22
SPECIFIC RELIGIOUS BELIEFS OF THE JAPANESE, 1994
(percent)

Question: Which of the following do you believe in?

Buddha	44
God	35
Teaching of the Bible or sutras	6
Power of amulets or charms	16
The afterworld or heaven	13
Miracles	13
Fortune-tellers or prophets	6
Nothing that relates to religion	24
Not sure/no response	7

Question: Do you think your soul exists even after death or not?

Exists after death	36
Does not exist	30
It is difficult to say	34

SOURCE: For top panel, survey by NHK, May 1994. For bottom panel, survey by the *Yomiuri Shimbun*, June 1994.

When I met him, almost a year before he was shot, he explained this view. It was important, he said, "that the Japanese accept responsibility for their savage behavior during the war." And responsibility was a question of morality. And morality was a matter of religion. The problem with the Japanese was that "they worship nature. But they have no religious or philosophical moral basis.

"In Europe," he [Motoshima] went on, "people's feelings are based upon centuries of philosophy and religion, for the Japanese only [the] worship [of] nature. This is what they have internalized. In a world ruled by nature, the question of individual responsibility doesn't come up."

He sounded like a character in a novel by Endo Shusaku, the Catholic author, much admired by Graham Greene. Endo, like the mayor, believed that his animistic countrymen lacked a

---

15. Ibid., pp. 254–55.

TABLE 4–23
RELIGIOSITY IN JAPAN, 1979–1995
(percent)

Question: [Do you agree or disagree] Religion is necessary for a happy life? Do you have any religious affiliation?

	Religion Is Necessary for a Happy Life	Have a Religious Affiliation
July 1979	46	34
July 1984	44	29
September 1989	38	28
June 1994	34	26
June 1995	26	20

SOURCE: Surveys by the *Yomiuri Shimbun*, latest that of June 1995.

bedrock of morality, a sense of good and evil.[15]

Discussions of the development of individualism from the seventeenth century on in the West have often stressed the economic roots (such as property rights) and the political (the claims for popular control of government through the mechanism of one person, one vote). In fact, in the American experience, religious individualism preceded economic and political individualism. It was the religious idea of each soul's being equal before God, and thereby each person's demanding deep respect by earthly society, that shaped the early insistence on individual rights. Tocqueville argues in the first volume of *Democracy in America* that the world's first true democracy emerged in seventeenth- and eighteenth-century New England out of such religious impulses:

> The immigrants, or as they so well named themselves, the Pilgrims, belonged to that English sect whose austere principles had led them to be called Puritans. Puritanism was not just a religious doctrine; in many respects it shared the most absolute democratic and republican theories. That was the element which had aroused its most dangerous adversaries. Persecuted by the home government, and with their strict principles offended by the everyday ways of the society in which they lived, the Puritans sought a land so barbarous and neglected by the

world that there at last they might be able to live in their own way and pray to God in freedom. . . .

[I]t is the [Puritans'] provisions for public education which, from the very first, throw into clearest relief the originality of American civilization.

The Code [Connecticut Code of 1650, promulgated by the colony's Puritan assembly] states: "It being one chief project of that old deluder, Satan, to keep men from the knowledge of the scriptures, as in former times, keeping them in an unknown tongue, so in these latter times, by persuading them from the use of tongues, so that at least, the true sense and meaning of the original might be clouded with false glosses of saint-seeming deceivers; and that learning may not be buried in the grave of our forefathers, in church and commonwealth, the Lord assisting our endeavors. . . ." Provisions follow establishing schools in all townships, and obliging the inhabitants, under penalty of heavy fines, to maintain them. In the same way, high schools are founded in the more densely populated districts. The municipal officials are bound to see that parents send their children to the schools, and can impose fines on those who refuse to do so; if the parents remain recalcitrant, society can take over the charge of the children from the family, depriving the parents of those natural rights which they abused. No doubt the reader has noticed the preamble to these regulations; in America it is religion which leads to enlightenment and the observance of divine law which leads men to liberty.[16]

We have been exploring Japan's course in developing sociopolitical individualism—an intellectual tradition that observers agree was singularly absent in the country at the end of World War II. From the above discussion it seems evident that the increasing recognition of individual claims that polls have been recording in postwar Japanese experience, especially between 1975 and 1995, has roots considerably different from the earlier American variety. In particular, the emergent Japanese individualism seems to be more explicitly located in the socioeconomy of advanced industrialism, rather than in a religiously inspired recognition of individual moral equality.

---

16. Alexis de Tocqueville, *Democracy in America* [George Lawrence translation, edited by J. P. Mayer] (New York: Harper and Row, 1969), pp. 36, 45.

TABLE 4–24
AMERICAN AND JAPANESE NORMS OF SEXUAL CONDUCT, 1994
(percent)

Question: If a man and woman have sex relations before marriage, do you think it is . . . ?

Americans	
Always/almost always wrong	35
Wrong only sometimes	20
Not wrong at all	42

Question: Do you think it is unacceptable or acceptable for unmarried men and women to have sexual relations with others?

Japanese	
Unacceptable	38
Acceptable	54

Question: What is your opinion about a married person having sexual relations with someone other than the marriage partner—is it . . . ?

Americans	
Always/almost always wrong	89
Wrong only sometimes	7
Not wrong at all	2

Question: Do you think it is unacceptable or acceptable for married men and women to have sexual relations with people other than their spouses?

Japanese	
Unacceptable	84
Acceptable	8

Question: What about sexual relations between two adults of the same sex—do you think it is . . . ?

Americans	
Always/almost always wrong	71
Wrong only sometimes	6
Not wrong at all	24

Question: Do you think it is unacceptable or acceptable for men and women to have sexual relations with someone of the same sex?

Japanese	
Unacceptable	75
Acceptable	11

NOTE: Not all response categories are shown.
SOURCE: Surveys by National Opinion Research Center (U.S.), February–May 1994, and NHK (Japan), June 1994.

TABLE 4–25
JAPANESE PREFERENCES IN WORK RELATIONSHIPS, 1973 AND 1994
(percent)

Question: If you were to be involved in a rather difficult long-term project, which of the following persons would you choose as your co-worker?

	1973	1994
A somewhat unfriendly person of high ability	27	25
A friendly person of low ability	68	71

NOTE: Not all response categories are given.
SOURCE: Surveys by NHK, latest that of 1994.

Social Relations

In general, the big differences in the area of social relations in the two countries are not those involving stated norms of ethical conduct. When, for example, the National Opinion Research Center (NORC) in the United States and NHK in Japan explored in 1994 questions of what is proper in sexual conduct, they found few differences in the stated norms in the two countries. In both, premarital sex receives markedly less disapproval than in the past. At the same time, on the question of married persons' having sexual relations with partners other than their marriage partners, the stated norm that it is always or almost always wrong, or unacceptable, remains firmly in place. Sexual relations between two adults of the same sex are deemed wrong by comparably large majorities in both countries (table 4–24).

The big differences in the two countries' social relations involve the persisting preference of Japanese for less adversarial, more cooperative interaction in domestic society as against Americans' individualistic assertiveness. Japanese norms in this area are nicely shown by questions asked by NHK in 1973 and repeated in 1994. If you had to be engaged in a demanding, long-term project, the survey asked, would you rather have as your co-worker "a somewhat unfriendly person of high ability" or "a friendly person of low ability?" In 1973, roughly seven respondents in ten favored the friendly person of low ability—cooperation over conflict. The proportions were virtually identical twenty years later (table 4–25).

TABLE 4–26

AMERICAN AND JAPANESE SENSE OF ACCOMPLISHMENT, 1990–1993
(percent)

Question: We are interested in the way people are feeling these days.
During the past few weeks, did you ever feel . . . ?

| | *Percent Responding "Yes"* | |
	Americans	Japanese
Particularly excited or interested in something	68	28
Proud because someone had complimented you on something you had done	70	20
Pleased about having accomplished something	84	37

SOURCE: World Values Survey, 1990–1993.

We see another variant of these preferences in the data shown in table 4–26. Americans are vastly more inclined than the Japanese to say they have been "particularly excited or interested in something," "pleased about having accomplished something," or "proud that they had been complimented on some accomplishment." Asked to assess the sharp differences shown in the table, our Japanese colleagues in the project suggested that the Japanese people are much more inclined to work in groups rather than individually. In this setting, there is a tendency to avoid giving credit to specific individuals within the groups. It is rare, our colleagues observed, for people outside the group to know who is in charge within it, or who has taken initiative in projects that have been completed. Japanese individuals are less likely to be recognized in terms of the success of a job than Americans often are. Beyond this, in areas of social interaction outside of work—such as weddings or family gatherings—social norms emphasize following precedent or tradition. As a result, individual persons are unlikely to receive compliments for the way they have handled these events. Complimenting other individuals is just another dimension of life in an individualistic society—a condition the United States still reflects more than does Japan.

CHAPTER 5

Polity and Political Values

While still under the American occupation in 1951, respondents in Japan were asked by the *Yomiuri Shimbun* whether or not the occupation "has been beneficial" to the country. An extraordinary 93 percent said that it had been beneficial, only 1 percent that it had not. As is obvious from the responses, large majorities of every social group made this positive assessment. In other questions, majorities or large pluralities said that workers had benefited (55 percent that they had, only 6 percent that they had not), that farmers had benefited (56 percent to 4 percent), and that business managers had benefited (33 percent to 9 percent). More than three decades later, respondents in both the United States and Japan were asked whether Japan had gained from changes the United States had imposed after World War II. Large majorities in Japan as well as in the United States in these CBS News/*New York Times*/Tokyo Broadcasting System polls saw Japan as having benefited. In February 1989, 73 percent of Japanese respondents called the overarching effects helpful. In the July 1985 survey, more Japanese volunteered that establishing democracy was the main benefit than said anything else—including the rebuilding of the country. (Americans were more likely to say that our assistance in rebuilding Japan was the principal benefit.)

Asked in the July 1985 CBS/NYT/TBS survey what comes to mind when you hear the words "the United States," the Japanese cited one or another related elements of the American political tradition— freedom, democracy, liberty, equality. A decade later in March 1995, in the survey collaboration involving the *Wall Street Journal* and the *Nihon Keizai Shimbun* (WSJ/NKS), more Japanese said they admired U.S. world leadership than selected any of five other attributes, but admiration for the U.S. political system ranked second. It surpassed cultural contributions, technological achievements, economic success, and national unity. In a November 1975 NHK survey, when asked about images of prewar and postwar Japan, a solid majority said "freedom" was an image of postwar Japan (54 percent), while only 4 percent identified the prewar Japanese experience this way.

It should be noted that democratic ideas do have substantial roots in Japan. For almost sixty years after the Meiji restoration (1868), Japan had a limited parliamentary system. Japan-watcher Ellen Frost makes the point that during the late nineteenth century the country's intellectuals debated the alternative merits of a constitutional monarchy or a more democratic system. But many concluded that Japan, by this time determined to catch up with the West economically, had no time "to waste" on the development of a pluralistic system that to many seemed undisciplined. Antidemocratic forces grew in strength, and the worldwide depression of the late 1920s and 1930s accentuated this impulse. The militarists gained control and Japan moved to war.[1]

The democratic ideas and practices imposed by the American occupation between 1946 and 1952 were not, then, entirely alien to Japan. Still, that country's transformation may be one of the most extraordinary and swift of any in modern history. A month after the Japanese surrendered, the "bill of rights" directive was issued by the supreme commander of Allied Forces, Douglas MacArthur, guaranteeing freedom of speech, assembly, religion, and political activity. Other reforms focused on demilitarization, land reform, and decentralization of the economy. A new constitution was drafted, fundamentally altering the political structure. It established representative democracy. In a 1952 survey done by the *Asahi Shimbun*, just 14 percent of respondents said they had read thoroughly their country's then five-year-old constitution, 19 percent that they had read it partially, and 67 percent that they had not read it at all. Even so, the basic idea of democratic institutions received broad endorsement.

Women were granted the vote for the first time during the U.S. occupation reforms. Incidentally, they received the franchise the same year—1946—that French women first got the vote. In Japan, laws that discriminated against women were abolished during the occupation. A mail survey taken by the *Mainichi Shimbun* in 1947 found 65 percent of Japanese respondents declaring themselves in

---

1. See Ellen L. Frost, *For Richer, for Poorer: The New U.S.-Japan Relationship* (Council on Foreign Relations, 1987), pp. 116–18.

favor of formal abolition of the inequality of the sexes in the civil code, while 32 percent were opposed. Not surprisingly, men were less in favor of these changes than women, though a majority of all groups favored the legal move toward equality. Japan's educational system was massively restructured as well.

One of the most difficult questions in postwar Japan was what to do about the emperor. Pollsters probed the public's views about this extensively. In 1946 the emperor formally renounced his claim to divinity. A survey taken by the *Yomiuri Shimbun* in 1948 found an over-whelming majority (90 percent) of the public favoring the "emperor system," defined here as retaining the emperor as the "wish of the people" and "the symbol of the nation." A question posed in 1954 by Yoron Kagaku Kyokai asked whether the emperor should be the sym-bol of the nation, or the actual head in some governmental sense of the country, or whether the position should be abolished entirely. A large majority (62 percent) favored keeping the emperor as a nation-al symbol, while 22 percent thought he should be the head of state. Just 1 percent wanted the emperor system entirely abolished. (It is worth noting here that for all the buffeting the British monarchy has taken in recent years, public backing for maintaining the monarchy remains strong. In an October 1995 poll taken by British Gallup, only 13 percent wanted to see the monarchy "abolished and replaced by a non-executive figurehead president like the ones they have in some continental countries," though many in the poll wanted to see it reformed.)

On the occasion of Emperor Hirohito's death in 1989, the CBS/NYT/TBS consortium asked the Japanese to assess the emper-or system. A near majority (49 percent) in the February poll indicat-ed that they strongly supported the system in its present form, 28 percent that they supported it but not strongly; only 20 percent declared themselves somewhat or strongly opposed. In this survey a very large majority (70 percent) rejected the prewar idea that the emperor was a human god, but 20 percent still expressed allegiance to this idea. Among persons sixty-five years old and older, 40 percent accepted the emperor as a human god.

Virtually every aspect of Japanese society was changed in at least some significant way during the American occupation of the country. These changes were imposed on a people devastated by war, and on a society where the group, rather than the individual, had long been the focal point of social organization and responsibility. Against this backdrop, the extent of the change toward democratic norms that present-day Japan manifests seems to us easily to be the overriding story. That there would be limits imposed by history and tradition, and areas where the adaptation to the new order seems to many individual Japanese to be inadequate, is in our view inevitable.

There can be no doubt but that the democratic ideal is highly valued in both countries. Since one clearly could not make that claim for the Japan that entered World War II, that it can now be made fairly points to an extraordinary evolution of the Japanese political system. The American occupation initiated many of these changes, but only the Japanese could have carried them ahead to their present reality.

Thinking about the Nation

This said, Americans and Japanese continue to differ substantially in political position and outlook. We see these differences in the way citizens of each country evaluate their respective countries. The Japanese polity is still engaged in establishing democratic institutions and traditions—while the United States has operated with them for more than two centuries. In addition, present-day Japan grapples with the issue of the country's responsibility for World War II and for atrocities committed during the war by the Japanese military—seen in the debate over whether the government should formally apologize, and in what words, for the country's role in the war. Both Japanese and German national feelings were obviously pummeled by the experience of the war, defeat, and postwar occupation.[2]

Surveys show the effects of these contrasting experiences. In a five-nation survey done by Gallup for the *Yomiuri Shimbun* in the spring of 1995, only distinct minorities of respondents in the United States, Japan, the United Kingdom, and France said they were *not* proud of their nation (a significantly larger 22 percent of Germans felt that way). But Americans differed from the Japanese and those in the other countries as well in the intensity of the pride they expressed. Seventy-three percent of Americans, compared with just 47 percent of Japanese, said they took great pride in their nationality (table 5–1). G. K. Chesterton famously observed that "America is the only nation in the world that is founded on a creed."[3] Americans'

---

2. Ian Buruma discusses this with great insight in *The Wages of Guilt: Memories of War in Germany and Japan* (New York: Meridian, 1995).

3. Chesterton made his observations in a brilliant book first published in 1922. G. K. Chesterton, *What I Saw in America* (New York: Da Capo Press, 1968; first published 1922), p. 7.

TABLE 5–1
American, Japanese, and Other Nationalities' National Pride, 1995
(percent)

Question: How much do you take pride in the fact that you are (American/Japanese/British/German/French)?

	Strongly	Somewhat	Not
American	73	23	2
Japanese	47	44	7
British	47	36	12
German	16	48	22
French	47	40	8

NOTE: Not all response categories are shown.
SOURCE: Survey by the Gallup Organization and the *Yomiuri Shimbun*, May 1995.

long-standing adherence to our political-idea system, along with our sense of the moral soundness of the ideas, together explain much of the unusual national pride that Americans express—often to the dismay of citizens of other countries.

Similar differences in professed national pride were found by the World Values Study Group in its World Values Survey (1990–1993). Asked "how proud are you to be [American/Japanese], 74 percent in the United States, as against just 27 percent in Japan, said they were very proud (table 5–2). Part of this huge difference can be attributed to a characteristic we have noted in many instances in this book—the inclination of many Japanese to take softer, less "extreme" responses. Younger respondents in both countries were less inclined than their elders to describe themselves as "very" proud. Still, 32 percent of all Japanese respondents said they were not proud of their national identity, compared with just 2 percent of Americans, and these differences are largest among the youngest respondents. Forty-two percent of those aged eighteen–twenty-nine in Japan said they were not proud to be Japanese, while only 2 percent of young Americans said this about their own national identity. The impact of the war and defeat, and the subsequent groping for a new political identity, seem clearly to have weakened the professed pride and confidence of many Japanese.

This effect is most evident, not surprisingly, on the question of whether, should another war ensue, a respondent would "be willing

TABLE 5–2
NATIONAL PRIDE IN AMERICA AND JAPAN, 1990–1993
(percent)

Question: How proud are you to be (American/Japanese) . . . ?

	Very Proud	Quite Proud	Not
All Americans	74	23	2
All Japanese	27	35	32
Americans, by age			
18–29 years	69	27	2
30–39 years	69	27	3
40–49 years	67	30	3
50–59 years	80	18	2
60–69 years	87	13	0
70 years and older	85	14	1
Japanese, by age			
18–29 years	27	35	42
30–39 years	21	33	38
40–49 years	22	42	31
50–59 years	36	36	21
60 years and older	45	23	23

NOTE: Not all response categories are shown.
SOURCE: World Values Survey, 1990–1993.

to fight for [his or her] country." Seventy percent of Americans said they would, as against 19 percent who said that they would not and 11 percent that they were not sure. In striking contrast, only 10 percent of Japanese said they would be willing to fight for their country, while 41 percent said they would not and 49 percent expressed doubt. Again, the differences are largest between the younger adults of the two societies (table 5–3).

Political Satisfaction and Dissatisfaction

Since the country's democratic institutions are relatively new and still evolving, it is not surprising that Japanese are much less inclined than Americans to express satisfaction with the way democracy is working in their country (table 5–4). Citizens of the United States

TABLE 5–3
PACIFISM IN AMERICANS AND JAPANESE, 1990–1993
(percent)

Question: Of course, we all hope that there will not be another war, but if it were to come to that, would you be willing to fight for your country?

	Yes	No	Don't Know
All Americans	70	19	11
All Japanese	10	41	49
Americans			
18–29 years	70	17	13
30–39 years	69	20	10
40–49 years	67	20	13
50–59 years	78	14	8
60–69 years	75	16	8
70 years and older	65	25	10
Japanese			
18–29 years	4	48	48
30–39 years	4	49	47
40–49 years	13	37	50
50–59 years	13	37	50
60 years and older	21	29	51

NOTE: Percentages may not add to 100 because of rounding.
SOURCE: World Values Survey, 1990–1993.

make many complaints about the current performance of their political system.[4] Nonetheless, Americans are generally more inclined to express confidence in their central political and economic institutions than are the Japanese (table 5–5). The issue of governmental corruption, in particular, finds citizens of Japan vastly more pessimistic or cynical than Americans (table 5–6). Recent polls taken by NHK and by the *Yomiuri Shimbun* in Japan have found only a fifth to

---

4. The authors have reviewed at length poll findings on the scope and substance of such complaints, especially in the pages of the *Public Perspective* and, formerly, *Public Opinion* magazines. See, for example, most recently, "Polity Watch," *Public Perspective*, vol. 6, no. 3, pp. 50–52. See also Ladd, "Is America Ready for a New Major Party?" *Chronicle of Higher Education*, November 24, 1995.

TABLE 5–4
AMERICAN AND JAPANESE SATISFACTION WITH DEMOCRACY, 1995
(percent)

Question: How satisfied are you with the way democracy works in this country . . . ?

	Satisfied	Mixed	Dissatisfied
All Americans	64	8	27
All Japanese	35	31	33
Young Americans (18–29 years)	54	13	34
Young Japanese (18–29 years)	29	44	26

NOTE: Percentages may not add to 100 because of rounding.
SOURCE: Surveys by the Gallup Organization, April 1995.

a fourth of respondents describing themselves as satisfied with "the current political situation" (table 5–7).

Surveys taken in both countries show large numbers of citizens expressing some measure of distrust about the national government. Still, the proportion of Japanese saying they can *never* "trust the government in Tokyo to do what is right" is higher by fivefold than that of Americans thus criticizing the government in Washington (table 5–8). Similarly, while Americans are significantly more inclined at present than they were in the 1950s and 1960s to criticize governmental officials as indifferent to their concerns, the level of concern about political unresponsiveness seems even greater in Japan (table 5–9).

Political Ideology

As we noted in the introduction to this volume, there is little dispute concerning the distinctive features of American political ideology, though there has been and continues to be extensive debate on the normative side—that is, whether the ideology should be praised for its elevation of individuals and individual choice, or condemned for encouraging an ideal of extreme, dysfunctional individual autonomy, and for blunting essential communitarian or collective impulses. A stream of nineteenth-century European visitors to the United States offered criticism frequently from the vantage point of the values of a

TABLE 5–5
PERCENTAGE OF AMERICANS AND JAPANESE WITH A "GREAT DEAL" OR
"QUITE A LOT" OF CONFIDENCE IN CENTRAL INSTITUTIONS, 1990–1993
(percent)

Question: How much confidence do you have in . . . ?

	All Americans	All Japanese	Young Americans (18–29 years)	Young Japanese (18–29 years)
Police	74	58	73	47
Legal system	57	61	55	49
Education system	55	45	57	35
Major companies	51	27	54	22
Armed forces	48	24	50	16
Congress/Diet	45	29	46	18

SOURCE: World Values Survey, 1990–1993

more differential, ascriptive class society.[5] Alexis de Tocqueville saw many positive dimensions of American individualism, as well as many negative, and his penetrating assessment has continued to attract readers. Charles Dickens was one of the first European visitors to criticize the American ideology and values from a more "modern" perspective—what he saw as the narrow, money-grubbing, and excessively materialistic bent of the populace.[6]

Today, critics such as Robert Bellah stress the "dark side" of contemporary American individualism.[7] Communitarians like Amitai Etzioni see a pressing need to rebuild institutions and values of the community in a sociopolitical climate made hostile by excessive individualism.[8] Some black intellectuals attack the ideology for its rejec-

---

5. See, for example, Frances Trollope, *Domestic Manners of the Americans*, Donald Smalley, ed. (Gloucester, Mass: Peter Green reprint, 1974, of Alfred A. Knopf edition [New York: 1949]; first published 1832); Anthony Trollope, *North America*, Donald Smalley and Bradford Booth, eds. (1986 DaCapo reprint of 1951 Knopf edition); and Hugo Münsterberg, *American Traits: From the Point of View of a German* (Boston: Houghton, Mifflin, 1902), pp. 146–49.
6. Charles Dickens, *American Notes for General Circulation* (Harmondsworth, England: Penguin Books, Ltd., 1972; first published in 1842).
7. Robert Bellah et al., *Habits of the Heart* (Berkeley, Calif.: University of California Press, 1985), p.142.
8. See the quarterly, founded and edited by Amitai Etzioni, *The Responsive Community* (Washington, D.C.: George Washington University).

TABLE 5–6
PERCEPTIONS OF CORRUPTION AS NORMAL IN THE UNITED STATES AND
JAPAN, 1989 AND 1992
(percent)

Question: Do you think corruption in government is part of the way
things work in the (United States/Japan), or do you think the government can run without corruption?

	Part of the Way Things Work	Possible Without
June 1989		
Americans	48	47
Japanese	83	16
December 1992		
Americans	45	51
Japanese	75	22

NOTE: Not all response categories are shown.
SOURCE: Surveys by CBS News/*New York Times* (U.S.) and the Tokyo Broadcasting System (Japan), latest that of December 1992.

tion of traditional African political values, which stress the collectivity.[9]
Yet for all the lumps it has taken, the American ideology, centered
around this notably far-reaching emphasis on individual rights and
individual responsibilities, remains as dominant today as it was in the
America of 1795.[10] Historian Louis Hartz called the ideology a "mono-
lith," and it remains a large, looming, impenetrable presence.[11]

But if America's ideological present essentially repeats its past,
and its future promises more of the same, the Japanese ideological
condition is far more confused and confusing. Japan entered World

---

9. See, for example, a paper written by Daryl Harris, "The Duality Complex: An Unre-
solved Paradox in African-American Politics," September 1995.
10. For review of survey data demonstrating the continuance of pervasive American
endorsement of the central values of the ideology, see Everett Ladd, *The American Ideology: An Exploration of the Origins, Meaning, and Role of American Political Ideas* (Storrs,
Conn.: The Roper Center for Public Opinion Research, 1994); and Everett Ladd,
"The Twentysomethings: Generation Myths Revisited," *Public Perspective,* January–February, 1995, pp. 14–18.
11. Hartz made this observation as part of a far-reaching and insightful examination
of American ideological development, *The Liberal Tradition in America* (New York:
Harcourt, Brace and World, 1964).

TABLE 5–7
Degree of Satisfaction with the Political Situation
in Japan, 1976–1995
(percent)

Question: Are you satisfied or dissatisfied with the current political situation?

	NHK		Yomiuri	
	Satisfied	Dissatisfied	Satisfied	Dissatisfied
1976	31	65	—	—
1977	36	54	—	—
1978	38	52	—	—
1980	23	71	—	—
1981	30	62	—	—
1982	28	64	—	—
1983	32	60	—	—
1984	34	59	—	—
1985	39	54	46	50
1986	46	47	61	36
1987	34	59	—	—
1988	38	55	43	52
1989	17	78	20	77
1990	42	54	44	53
1991	37	57	43	55
1992	24	71	33	65
1993	15	81	19	79
1994	26	70	19	79
1995	29	67	22	73

NOTES: Not all response categories are shown.
SOURCE: Surveys by NHK and the *Yomiuri Shimbun*.

War II as a most extraordinary amalgam of tradition and modernity. On the one hand, it bore the imprint of the institutions and values of feudal society. On the other, its ruling elites had committed the country to catching up with the West, and under their leadership, Japan had become a major industrial nation. The traditional social structure and values of ascriptive class societies, and the economic organization of industrialism, have typically been like oil and water— unmixable, competitive, and hostile traditions. All across Europe, for

TABLE 5–8

DEGREE OF TRUST IN THE GOVERNMENT IN THE UNITED STATES AND
JAPAN, 1989 AND 1992

(percent)

Question: How much of the time do you think you can trust the government in (Washington/Tokyo) to do what is right—just about always, most of the time, only some of the time, or never?

	Always	Most of the Time	Some of the Time	Never
June 1989				
Americans	4	31	57	6
Japanese	1	23	46	30
December 1992				
Americans	2	24	64	8
Japanese	1	14	44	40

NOTE: Percentages may not add to 100 because of rounding.
SOURCE: Surveys by CBS News/*New York Times* (U.S.) and the Tokyo Broadcasting System (Japan), latest that of December 1992.

example, aristocracies aligned themselves against industrial development, which was gradually achieved under middle-class leadership over their stubborn resistance. Aristocracies radiated contempt for the norms and practices of bourgeois society.

In Japan, however, the rush to economic modernity was led by a segment of the leadership of the old, aristocratic order. Political sociologist Seymour Martin Lipset has described the uniqueness of this aspect of the Japanese experience of economic development:

Japan and the United States are two of the foremost examples of industrial success in the contemporary world, and they took very different paths to reach that position. Efforts to account for America's past success have emphasized that as compared to Europe, it had fewer encrusted pre-industrial traditions to overcome, and in particular, that it had never been a feudal or hierarchical state church–dominated society. All of Europe and, of course, Japan as well were once feudal, organized in terms of monarchy, aristocracy and fixed hierarchy, with a value system embedded in religious institutions

114

TABLE 5–9
Degree of Satisfaction with Responsiveness of Government in the United States and Japan, 1952–1994
(percent)

Question: How well do you think Japanese people's opinions are reflected in national policies?

	Very/Somewhat Well	Not Very/Not at All Well
Japanese		
1982	23	63
1983	30	53
1984	33	50
1985	36	45
1986	32	53
1987	35	52
1988	26	63
1989	32	58
1990	29	58
1991	31	60
1992	23	69
1993	30	61
1994	24	67

Question: I don't think public officials care much what people like me think.

	Disagree	Agree
Americans		
1952	63	35
1956	71	26
1960	73	25
1964	62	36
1966	57	34
1968	55	43
1970	50	47
1972	49	49
1974	46	50
1976	44	51
1978	45	51
1980	44	52
1982	50	47
1984	57	42
1986	43	52
1988	38	51
1990	23	64
1992	38	52
1994	23	66

NOTE: Not all response categories are shown.
SOURCES: For top panel, surveys by the Prime Minister's Office, latest that of December 1994. For bottom panel, the University of Michigan, latest that of 1994.

that both emphasized the virtues inherent in agrarian society and deprecated commercial activities. . . . [Yet] the interpretation which identifies post-feudal structures and values as antithetical to the development of modern industrial society is challenged by the history of Japan. . . . Rising from a terrible military defeat and the almost total destruction of its economy, Japan experienced a level of sustained economic growth which enabled it both to become, in per capita terms, one of the wealthiest countries in the world and to compete successfully with the United States. But this post-war "miracle" continues a successful development pattern that began in the latter part of the nineteenth century long after Northern Europe and North America started their industrial revolutions. . . . Japan is the earliest non-Western country which became affluent and industrially developed. . . .

Japan has modernized economically while retaining many aspects of its pre-industrial feudal culture. Until the mid-nineteenth century, the social structure under the Tokugawa Shogunate was still feudal; its culture still resembled that of Renaissance Europe. Japan was an extremely hierarchical society which placed a tremendous emphasis on obligation to those higher up as well as to those down below. . . . Until the mid-nineteenth century, Japan had avoided a prolonged breakdown of feudalism, but the Japanese aristocratic elite decided that the country had to industrialize to escape being conquered by the imperialist West. Determined to avoid dependence on or take-over by the Western powers, this elite sought to remake the country economically along Western lines. . . . Few Westerners, other than scholars, are knowledgeable about the reorganization of Japan. The record of the country's mid-nineteenth century barons, that brilliant group of oligarchs who took over the country determined to modernize it, makes that of any group of communist rulers seem like one of indifferent bumblers. The changes which occurred in Japan from the 1860s on were among the most remarkable societal transformations that have ever occurred. The barons carried through a sociological transformation, using Emperor Meiji to legitimize it.[12]

---

12. Lipset's summary of these and related developments is the best available. See his "American Exceptionalism: Japanese Uniqueness," in *American Exceptionalism: A Double-edged Sword* (New York: W.W. Norton, 1996), pp. 211–13. Many other scholars

In the United States, then, with the successful completion of the war for independence from England in the late eighteenth century, the old aristocratic leadership was entirely displaced and the country's development—including, of course, its economy—took place under the direction of middle-class leadership entirely committed to modern social values of individualism and egalitarianism. Japan differs fundamentally, in that its governing elite during the nineteenth-century transformation sprang from the old order and made a conscious effort to maintain large elements of traditional society even as they rushed to economic modernity. Thus, as Lipset observes, "the Japanese have continued to uphold values and institutions which, from the perspective of Western market economic analysis, make little sense. They maintain a society in which deference and hierarchy are important. . . . In theory, the person does not exist as an individual, but only as a member of certain large groups: family, school, community, company, nation. . . . [T]he Japanese do not want to stand out as individuals."[13]

This exceptional Japanese path of social development—as pronouncedly different from the common patterns of transition from ascriptive class to egalitarian social systems in its own way as the American path is in another—forms an essential part of the backdrop for present-day Japanese sociopolitical ideology. At the same time, one should not minimize the pressures toward a more far-reaching and complete sociopolitical individualism accruing from the basic social structure of postindustrial society. Postindustrialism means, among other things, vast increases in formal education, with all that that

---

have, of course, examined these developments. See, for example, Sakata Yoshio, "The Beginning of Modernization in Japan," in Ardath W. Burks, ed., *The Moderniz-ers* (Boulder, Colo.: Westview Press, 1985), pp. 69–83. See also Marius B. Jansen, ed., *Changing Japanese Attitudes toward Modernization* (Princeton: Princeton University Press, 1965); William W. Lockwood, ed., *The State and Economic-Enterprise in Japan* (Princeton: Princeton University Press, 1965); Ronald P. Dore, ed., *Aspects of Social Change in Modern Japan* (Princeton: Princeton University Press, 1967); Robert E. Ward, ed., *Political Development in Modern Japan* (Princeton: Princeton University Press, 1968); Donald Shively, ed., *Tradition and Modernization in Japanese Culture* (Princeton: Princeton University Press, 1971); James W. Morely, ed., *Dilemmas of Growth in Prewar Japan* (Princeton: Princeton University Press, 1971); Bernard S. Silberman and H.D. Harootunian, eds., *Japan in Crisis: Essays on Taisho Democracy* (Princeton: Princeton University Press, 1974); W. G. Beasley, *The Meiji Restoration* (Stanford: Stanford University Press, 1971). See Edwin O. Reischauer, *The Japanese* (Cambridge, Mass.: The Belknap Press, 1977), pp. 78–87; Robert J. Smith, *Japanese Society. Tradition, Self and the Social Order* (Cambridge, Mass.: Cambridge University Press, 1983), pp. 9–36.
13. Lipset, "American Exceptionalism: Japanese Uniqueness," p. 217.

implies for equalizing individual opportunity and heightening individual expectations. Similarly, the pervasive electronic communications of modern advanced industrial society break down the social-group insularity that was essential to maintaining hierarchy and deference in traditional society. In the economic sphere, the modern industrial order takes people out of the social setting that sustained every ascriptive class order—family-based and agricultural—and puts them in the far more impersonal world of factory and bureaucracy.

Any idea that long-established social norms would disappear quickly in the face of these individual-emphasizing pressures would contradict much that we have learned about the strength and persistence of cultural traditions. Conversely, any idea that the values of the old order could for the long term resist erosion in the face of a sociopolitical setting so profoundly hostile to them seems equally unrealistic. It seemed unrealistic to Alexis de Tocqueville, of course, who prophesied individualism's continuing march. We would expect modern-day Japan to reflect, then, significant elements of its own distinctive pattern in ideological development, along with continuing adaptations to greater sociopolitical individualism. And indeed, what we have found and have reported thus far seems entirely consistent with what these theoretical perspectives would lead us to expect.

Nihonjinron

Many commentators on modern Japan have noted the "*Nihonjinron* boom," especially as it has developed since the 1960s. The term refers to literature and argument that stress Japanese cultural uniqueness. Kazufumi Manabe and his colleagues have reviewed the *Nihonjinron* literature and conducted empirically based survey research to measure the level of familiarity the Japanese public has with it, and the extent to which the public subscribes to the argument's central claims. Manabe et al. note that "central to *Nihonjinron* are annunciations about what it means to be Japanese."[14]

---

14. Kazufumi Manabe, Harumi Befu, and Watanabe Fumio, "Japanese Cultural Nationalism: An Empirical Investigation of Nihonjinron" (1994), pp. 133–42; Manabe and Befu, An Empirical Investigation of Nihonjinron: The Degree of Exposure of Japanese to Nihonjinron Propositions and the Functions the Propositions Serve (part 1), Kwansei Gakuin University Annual Studies, 1989, vol. 38, pp. 35–62; and Manabe, Befu, and David McConnell, An Empirical Investigation of Nihonjinron: The Degree of Exposure of Japanese to Nihonjinron Propositions and the Functions These Propositions Serve (part 2), Kwansei Gakuin University Annual Studies, 1990, vol. 39, pp. 139–67.

Relatedly, they have explored the degree of perceived social distance between Japanese and foreigners—the extent to which foreigners are accepted in Japanese society. Their findings suggest that many of the claims about the force and unique character of Japanese "cultural nationalism" may be exaggerated. Japanese do have a strong sense of national cultural identity, but the findings of Manabe and his colleagues suggest many more similarities to other people's cultural nationalism than differences from it. Their research also suggests that younger Japanese are much less inclined to subscribe to the idea that they are somehow a "people apart" from others, or to impose unusual barriers to the acceptance of foreigners. The data suggest, in other words, that as Japan has become more "internationalized" through trade, travel, and pervasive electronic communication, younger people in particular have become less inclined than their elders to assert the idea of a unique Japaneseness.

From a perspective formed from extensive engagement in Japanese literature rather than empirical social science, Peter Dale is similarly suspicious about the extravagant claims of national difference made in the *Nihonjinron* literature.[15] Dale describes the *Nihonjinron* as a "commercialized expression of modern Japanese nationalism." He notes the huge volume of literature discussing the supposed uniqueness of Japanese identity, citing one survey, covering 1946 to 1978, which identified about 700 books on this theme, "a remarkable 25 percent of which were issued in the peak three-year period from 1976 to 1978." Dale argues that much of the literature is in fact not so much an attempt at careful description of what is as a prescription—an attempt to shape elements of national culture for certain political and economic ends:

> *Every inch of autonomous self-assertion by the individual is contested as threatening the hegemonic reach and authority of the corporate national ideal.* While intent on projecting an image of Japan's national uniqueness abroad, the Nihonjinron vigorously deny the very possibility of individual, uniquely personal identity within Japan itself.

Dale sees the main thrust of the literature, the purpose that it is promoting, as a profoundly dysfunctional one:

15. Peter N. Dale, *The Myth of Japanese Uniqueness* (New York: Saint Martin's Press, 1986), pp. 14–15.

Most disturbing of all is the fact that this fictive confounding of self and other rebuts and disclaims the possibility of love itself. In its stead, we find the impoverished ersatz of a disguised narcissism submerged beneath the disembodied image of a disindividualized collectivity, in which the idiom of identity is both tribal and anonymous.[16]

Other people's nationalisms, typically, are at least somewhat disturbing to those who stand outside them. Both America and Japan have historically manifested strong nationalisms—although those senses of national identity have profoundly different starting points. American nationalism is explicitly political—the idea of founding a nation not on blood or ethnicity but on a political creed. Japanese nationalism is more traditional in its emphasis on distinctive ethnic roots and attributes. American nationalism celebrates the idea of constructing a new nation out of a great variety of ethnic traditions— *e pluribus unum*. Again more conventionally, Japanese nationalism posits the idea of a singular people maintaining its singularity—*e unum unum*. Nonetheless, any suggestion that either American or Japanese nationalism sets the country outside of history—outside the normal bounds and conditions of social development and causality—is unsustainable. We see Japan as evolving from what is in fact a not-unusual ascriptive class structure, in which many norms, values, and institutions flourished much as they did across Western Europe and elsewhere on the planet. These institutions and values persisted longer in Japan than in Western Europe—and the rush to economic modernity was launched in ways designed to minimize the short-term disruption of such norms. This is indeed a distinct, if not literally unique, episode in the global process of economic modernization. The course does not suggest, however, that norms and behaviors associated with sociopolitical individualism either have been or will be suppressed in modern-day Japan.

The idea of Japanese uniqueness has produced a striking number of survey questions that the authors have not seen in their examination of other eastern and western countries. Louis Harris and the *Asahi Shimbun* asked in 1971 and again in 1982 whether Japanese culture was "something Westerners can grow to appreciate" or whether it is "generally outside their understanding." Majorities of Americans in both surveys thought Westerners could grow to understand Japan-

---

16. Ibid., p. 223 (emphasis added).

ese culture. In 1986 the question was broadened and respondents were asked whether they felt they understood Japanese society. Only about one in five said they did, but three-quarters said they did not. In the same survey about six in ten Americans said the Japanese did not understand American society. The Gallup surveys for the Japanese government have for many years asked how much understanding the Americans have of the Japanese. These surveys usually inquire about the trade and security relationship, and questions about levels of understanding may reflect those concerns. Pluralities or majorities of Americans have labeled the understanding of each other as "fair" as opposed to "good" or "poor." In February 1995, for example, 21 percent of Americans felt the understanding between Japan and America was good, 54 percent fair, and 23 percent poor.

Political Individualism

Individualism is corrosive of the idea of traditional, fixed social classes. The individualist idea is, inevitably, one of a "middle-class" society. It is important to note, then, that the Japanese public, like its American counterpart, by overwhelming majorities sees itself in the middle of a social order, and that the conscious identification as middle class has grown in both countries in the postwar period (table 5–10).

Americans do express a far stronger commitment to sociopolitical individualism today than do the Japanese—but then, Americans continue to stand out in this regard in all cross-national comparisons. Table 5–11 summarizes United States-Japan comparisons on this dimension, drawing on World Values Survey data. We see that Americans are much more inclined to take the position that individuals should take more responsibility in providing for themselves, rather than the position that the state should take more responsibility to ensure that everyone is provided for. Relatedly, Americans emphasize much more than do Japanese the idea of extending greater incentives for individual effort, rather than taking steps to make incomes more equal.

Looking at responses to survey questions in this substantive area by the age of respondents, we see that while younger Japanese are closer to their American counterparts in many of the routine practices of everyday life—areas such as workplace relationships and gender roles in the family—than are older Japanese and Americans, on the underlying norm of a highly individualized idea of freedom, young Japanese and Americans remain far apart and differ in roughly the same

TABLE 5–10
PERCEPTIONS OF CLASS IN THE UNITED STATES AND JAPAN, 1949–1995
(percent)

Question: To which of the following levels do you think your present living status belongs?

	Lower Class	Lower-middle Class	Middle-middle Class	Upper-middle Class	Upper Class
Japanese					
1958	17	32	37	3	a
1960	14	32	40	3	a
1965	8	28	50	7	1
1970	7	25	57	8	1
1975	5	23	59	7	1
1980	7	28	54	7	1
1985	8	28	54	6	1
1990	7	28	53	8	1
1995	5	24	57	10	1

Question: If you were asked to use one of four names for your social class, which would you say you belong to?

	Lower Class	Working Class	Middle Class	Upper Class
Americans				
1949	3	60	32	2
1972	6	47	44	2
1975	5	48	44	3
1980	5	46	45	3
1985	4	45	47	4
1990	4	46	47	3
1994	5	45	46	3

a. Less than 1%.
SOURCES: For top panel, surveys by the Prime Minister's Office, latest that of 1995. For bottom panel, National Opinion Research Center, latest that of February–May 1994.

TABLE 5–11
PREFERENCES FOR POLITICAL AND ECONOMIC INDIVIDUALISM IN THE UNITED STATES AND JAPAN, 1990–1993

Question: How would you place your views on this scale? 1 means you agree completely with the statement on the left, 10 means you agree completely with the statement on the right, or you can choose any number in between.

	Points 1–4	*Points 5–6*	*Points 7–10*
	Individuals should take more responsibility for providing for themselves		The state should take more responsibility to ensure everyone is provided for
Americans	70	16	13
Japanese	15	25	49
	Private ownership should be increased		Government ownership should be increased
Americans	72	19	8
Japanese	19	37	11
	Competition is good; it stimulates people to work hard and develop new ideas		Competition is harmful; it brings out the worst in people
Americans	76	14	10
Japanese	40	32	11
	Incomes should be more equal		There should be greater incentives for individual effort
Americans	21	22	58
Japanese	19	36	29

NOTE: For Americans, percentages may not add to 100 because of rounding. For Japanese, not all response categories are given.
SOURCE: World Values Survey, 1990–1993.

TABLE 5–12
PREFERENCES FOR FREEDOM OR EQUALITY IN THE UNITED STATES AND
JAPAN, 1995
(percent)

Question: Which of these two statements comes closest to your own opinion? . . . I find that both freedom and equality are important. But if I were to choose one or the other, I would consider personal freedom more important; that is, everyone can live in freedom and develop without hindrance. [or] . . . Certainly both freedom and equality are important. But if I were to choose one or the other, I would consider equality more important, that is, that nobody is underprivileged and that social class differences are not so strong.

	Freedom	Equality
All Americans	68	23
All Japanese	35	31
Young Americans (18–29 years)	63	29
Young Japanese (18–29 years)	35	33

Question: Do you agree or disagree with the following statement? . . . We are more likely to have a healthy economy if the government allows more freedom for individuals to do as they wish.

	Agree	Neither	Disagree
All Americans	43	22	32
All Japanese	12	33	21
Young Americans (18–29 years)	41	25	31
Young Japanese (18–29 years)	15	37	23

TABLE 5–12 (continued)

Question: Imagine two secretaries, of the same age, doing practically the same job. One finds out that the other earns $50 a week more than . . . [the other] does. The better paid secretary, however, is quicker, more efficient and more reliable. . . . In your opinion, is it fair or not fair that one secretary is paid more than the other?

	Fair	Unfair
All Americans	82	15
All Japanese	48	33
Young Americans (18–29 years)	80	18
Young Japanese (18–29 years)	44	38

NOTE: Not all response categories are shown.
SOURCE: Surveys by the Gallup Organization, April 1995.

magnitudes as do the entire populations of the two countries. Gallup posed an interesting question in a 1995 survey done in both countries, in which respondents were asked to assess two contrasting statements about freedom and equality (table 5–12). We see that 63 percent of Americans from eighteen to twenty-nine years of age chose the idea that "I would consider personal freedom more important, that is, everyone can live in freedom and develop without hindrance," over the opposing idea that "I would consider equality more important; that is, that nobody is underprivileged and that social class differences are not so strong." Only 35 percent of their Japanese age mates opted for the first of these two ideas or ideals. Similarly, young Japanese were far more inclined to the view that it is unfair that a less highly performing employee be paid less than a more achieving coworker in the same field (table 5–12). In short, like West Europeans in this regard, as Japanese political values have evolved in the direction of more individualism and democracy, the Japanese have continued to insist on far more softening of individualism through collective guarantees than the American public will accept.

American-style individualism involves not only commitment to the ideal of individual opportunity to develop one's self but also the sense that the individual can control his or her destiny. This has given much of the American public a self-confidence not seen in the

Japanese public. In a 1994 survey done by the Luntz Research Companies, 73 percent of respondents said that "as Americans we can always find a way to solve our problems." A virtually identical 74 percent said that "in America, if you work hard you can be anything you want to be." Indication of a very different level of self-confidence in Japan comes from a question posed in the World Values Survey. Seventy-six percent of Americans placed themselves at points 7 through 10 on a ten-point scale—indicating that they believed they had much freedom of choice and control over the way their lives turned out. Only 26 percent of Japanese put themselves at this high-confidence/high-control end of the continuum. Also in the World Values Survey, 57 percent in the United States, but just 27 percent in Japan, disagreed with the statement "if an unjust law were passed by government, I could do nothing about it."

As noted above, the more individualistic American public is less inclined to look to government than is the Japanese public. This difference appears in a great variety of questions, including a number where at first glance it might seem that something else is at issue. Consider, for example, the data in table 5–13—involving two questions posed in the 1994 International Social Survey Programme (ISSP), done in the United States and Japan as well as other countries. Only 18 percent of American women indicated strong agreement with the position that "families should receive financial benefits for child care when both parents work," a position taken by 46 percent of Japanese women. In all, 67 percent of Japanese women as against 49 percent of their U.S. counterparts endorsed financial benefits for child care. Americans are just less inclined to look to the state.

A question asked by NHK in a December 1993 survey reinforces this point. Seventy-six percent of Japanese respondents agreed that their government should be entirely responsible for social welfare; only 27 percent disagreed. Another question, posed in both countries in 1994 as part of the ISSP study, found only 10 percent of Japanese as against 51 percent of Americans agreeing with the statement that "private enterprise is the best way to resolve [the country's] economic problems."

Group Membership and Volunteerism

Tocqueville noted more than a century and a half ago that the strong American sense of individual efficacy, confidence, and responsibility had fostered an unusually vigorous associational life in the country. Recent empirical research done in the United States and other coun-

TABLE 5–13
AMERICAN AND JAPANESE VIEWS ON MATERNITY LEAVE AND CHILD CARE
BENEFITS, 1994
(percent)

Question: Do you agree or disagree that working women should
receive paid maternity leave when they have a baby?

	Strongly Agree	Agree
All Americans	28	46
All Japanese	86	8
American women	32	46
Japanese women	87	8

Question: Do you agree or disagree that families should receive
financial benefits for child care when both parents work?

All Americans	15	30
All Japanese	48	19
American women	18	31
Japanese women	46	21

NOTE: Not all response categories are shown.
SOURCE: Survey by the International Social Survey Programme (Japan),
1994.

tries confirms that Tocqueville's insightful description of this aspect
of U.S. life in the early nineteenth century still applies. That is, Americans are much more inclined to volunteer their time and money for
various civic and religious functions than are most other peoples.[17] In
1991, for example, 49 percent of Americans reported doing some
form of volunteer work in the past twelve months, as compared with
13 percent of Germans and 19 percent of French citizens. Twenty-
seven percent of Americans, compared with only 3 percent of Germans and 2 percent of French, indicated that they had done such voluntary activity for one or more religious organizations. For
educational activities, the three-country percentages (United

17. See "Democracy in America: How Are We Doing?" *Public Perspective*, March–April
1994, pp. 3–16.

States/Germany/France) are 15, 1, and 2. For environment-related work, the percentages are 9, 1, and 1.[18]

Americans are shown differing from Japanese in associational activity in much the same way as they differ from Europeans. We see (table 5–14) that a high 64 percent of Japanese are reported in the World Values Study as belonging to *no* voluntary organizations, the status of just 18 percent of Americans. Fourteen percent of Americans said they participated in some form of political party activity, as against just 2 percent of Japanese. These behavioral results applied even though Americans and Japanese expressed essentially the same (low) level of interest in politics. The pattern of greater U.S. involvement in group life held for every group examined in the World Values Survey except trade unions, where roughly the same proportions of Americans and Japanese said they had been involved. As the data in table 5–15 attest, the differences in associational activity shown for the entire populations of the two countries apply for men and women separately, and they are as great for the young as for the entire populace. For example, 9 percent of eighteen–to–twenty-nine-year-old Americans indicated participation in some form of political party activity, as against just 1 percent of young Japanese.

Social and Political Ethics

In some important areas, Americans and Japanese in the large make essentially the same distinctions regarding what's right and wrong. For example, 75 percent of Americans and 70 percent of Japanese responded in the World Values Study that "claiming government benefits which you are not entitled to" is something never justified. On the more personal side, two-thirds in both countries say that "lying in your own interest" is something entirely without justification. In considering these and other data in table 5–16, it is important to remember that people are being asked about what should be the norm—not whether they ever violate it. We believe that the norms people hold are important, and the fact that they are sometimes violated does not lessen their importance as background and guide in social practice. At the same time, these are some of the areas where the two peoples place quite different emphasis. For example, just 17 percent of Americans said that killing in self-defense is never justified—a position that 52 percent of Japanese interviewed in the

---

18. All of these data are from ibid.

TABLE 5–14
RATE OF AMERICAN AND JAPANESE PARTICIPATION IN VOLUNTARY
ORGANIZATIONS, 1990–1993
(percent)

Statement: Please look carefully at the following list of voluntary
organizations and activities and say which, if any, you belong to.

	Americans	Japanese
Religious or church organizations	47	7
Arts	20	6
Sports or recreation	21	9
None	18	64
Professional associations	15	4
Political parties or groups	14	2
Youth work (for example, scouts, guides, youth clubs, etc.)	12	a
Other groups	11	5
Trade unions	8	7
Conservation, the environment, ecology	8	1
Women's groups	8	3
Voluntary organizations concerned with health	7	a
Local community action on issues like poverty, employment, housing, racial equality	5	a
Animal rights	5	a
Third world development or human rights	2	a
Peace movement	2	a

a. Less than 1%.
SOURCE: World Values Survey, 1990–1993.

World Values Survey took. Using marijuana or hashish is described
as never justified by huge majorities in both countries, but by a substantially larger one in Japan (table 5–16). In the areas involving
value choice associated with Western religious traditions, Americans
are understandably the more inclined to proscribe certain activities.
We see this on the issue of married people's having sexual relations
outside the marriage.

We touch briefly on one area that showed little difference
between the people of Japan and America. Thirty-nine percent of
Americans and 34 percent of the Japanese took the position that
abortion could never be justified. Abortion is generally legal in Japan

TABLE 5–15
AMERICAN AND JAPANESE GROUP MEMBERSHIP BY SEX AND AGE, 1990–1993
(percent)

Statement: Please look carefully at the following list of voluntary organizations and activities and say which, if any, you belong to.

	Women's Groups	Political Groups	None
All Americans	8	14	18
All Japanese	3	2	64
American men	1	16	17
American women	15	12	19
Young Americans (18–29 years)	6	9	18
Japanese men	1	3	60
Japanese women	5	1	67
Young Japanese (18–29 years)	2	1	69

SOURCE: World Values Survey, 1990–1993.

and the United States, though in the United States some restrictions are placed on second- and third-trimester abortions, and individual states are able to limit the practice. These data and others show that significant numbers in both countries are troubled by the practice. The CBS/NYT/TBS survey in June 1989, for example, found 18 percent of Americans saying that abortion is "always" wrong, 65 percent saying that it is "sometimes" wrong, and 12 percent saying that it is "never" wrong. The numbers for the Japanese were 14 percent, 74 percent, and 3 percent, respectively. To digress a bit further on this subject, the World Values Survey found that majorities in both countries (86 percent in the United States, 94 percent in Japan) approved of abortion in a situation where "the mother's health is at risk by the pregnancy," that 54 percent of Americans but 75 percent of the Japanese approved "where it is likely that the child will be born physically handicapped." Only 29 percent of Americans, but 55 percent of Japanese, approved "when the woman is not married"; 26 percent of Americans and 48 percent of the Japanese approved "where a married couple does not want to have any more children."

TABLE 5–16
ACTS IDENTIFIED AS "NEVER JUSTIFIED" BY AMERICANS AND JAPANESE,
1990–1993
(percent)

Statement: Please tell me for each of the following statements whether you think it can always be justified, never be justified, or something in between.

	Americans	Japanese
Japanese more likely to say never justified		
Killing in self-defense	17	52
Keeping money that you have found	42	71
Using the drug marijuana or hashish	79	92
Avoiding a fare on public transportation	70	83
Cheating on tax if you have the chance	76	86
Failing to report damage you've done accidentally to a parked vehicle	75	85
Prostitution	66	75
Similar responses		
Threatening workers who refuse to join a strike	80	84
Buying something you knew was stolen	83	86
Taking and driving away a car belonging to someone else	92	92
Lying in your own interest	66	65
Homosexuality	56	61
Divorce	22	20
Throwing away litter in a public place	80	77
Political assassinations	79	75
Abortion	39	34
Claiming government benefits that you are not entitled to	75	70
Americans more inclined to say never justified		
Driving under the influence of alcohol	89	82

(table continues)

131

TABLE 5–16 (continued)

	Americans	Japanese
Sex under the legal age of consent	69	61
Suicide	69	60
Someone accepting a bribe in the cause of his duties	87	76
Fighting with police	59	47
Euthanasia terminating the life of the incurably sick	36	21
Married men/women having an affair	78	54

NOTE: Respondents were asked to rate each statement on a scale of 1 to 10, with 1 being "never justified" and 10 being "always justified." Responses shown = 1 and 2 on the scale.
SOURCE: World Values Survey, 1990–1993.

Current Politics

People in both countries express roughly the same levels of interest in politics. Sixteen percent in the United States, compared with 13 percent in Japan, describe politics as very important in their lives (table 5–17). Slightly more than a third in both countries called it quite important. Politics ranked behind such things as family, friends, work, and leisure in terms of being thought of as very important.

Fewer Japanese (6 percent) than Americans (14 percent) said that when they get together with friends they often discuss politics. Thirty percent in the United States and a comparable 33 percent in Japan say they never discuss politics at social occasions (table 5–17).

In one area of politics, somewhat curiously, Americans are much more inclined to say they pay a lot of attention than are Japanese— this involves news about the other country. We see that in every occasion when the question was asked over the past decade, far larger proportions of Americans—ranging from four-to-one to two-to-one—have said they usually pay a lot of attention to news about the other country (table 5–18).

As the authors finish this book, the 1996 U.S. presidential election campaign has begun. On November 5, 1996, people across the United States will elect a president, 33 senators, 435 representatives, and 11 governors. Hundreds of elections for state and local offices will be

TABLE 5–17
THE IMPORTANCE OF POLITICS TO AMERICANS AND JAPANESE, 1990–1993
(percent)

Statement: Please say for each of the following how important it is in your life . . .

	Politics Is Very Important	Quite Important	Not Very Important	Not at All Important
Americans	16	34	38	12
Japanese	13	36	38	3

Question: When you get together with friends, would you say you discuss political matters . . .

	Frequently	Occasionally	Never
Americans	14	56	30
Japanese	6	59	33

NOTE: Not all response categories are shown.
SOURCE: World Values Survey, 1990–1993.

held, too. As we have stressed throughout this book, the impressive continuity that this one hundred fifth national election represents is something of which Americans are justly proud. President Clinton, who won election four years ago with 43 percent of the popular vote, apparently will face no opposition in the Democratic party for renomination. Nine contenders are vying for the GOP nomination. Ross Perot, who garnered 19 percent of the vote in 1992, has not indicated clearly his intentions for 1996, but he and his supporters are working to establish a third political party.

Dissatisfaction with politics-as-usual has increased interest in a third party to challenge the Democrats and the Republicans. The number identifying themselves as political independents has risen substantially over the past half-century. In 1944, 77 percent of Americans said they identified with either the Democratic or Republican parties; only 16 percent called themselves independents. In late summer 1995, a still considerable 58 percent identified themselves with the major parties, but nearly 40 percent identified themselves as independents. In some surveys today, more people identify themselves as independents than as Democrats or Republicans. Movement away from the long-ruling governing party in Japan is also evi-

TABLE 5–18
AMOUNT OF ATTENTION AMERICANS AND JAPANESE PAY TO THE OTHER
COUNTRY, 1985–1994
(percent)

Question: How much attention do you usually pay to news about
(Japan/U.S.)—a lot, some, or not much?

	A Lot	Some	Not Much
Americans			
July 1985	26	39	35
May 1988	24	40	35
June 1990	29	45	25
Nov. 1991	29	44	27
Dec. 1992	22	47	31
June 1993	17	46	35
Dec. 1994	14	48	38
Japanese			
July 1985	6	51	39
May 1988	9	56	34
June 1990	7	53	38
Nov. 1991	9	46	43
Dec. 1992	7	55	38
June 1993	6	57	36
Dec. 1994	7	51	41

NOTE: Percentages may not add to 100 because of rounding.
SOURCE: Surveys by CBS News/*New York Times* (U.S.) and the Tokyo Broadcasting System (Japan), latest that of December 1994.

dent, though as we have stressed earlier, the sources of popular discontent appear to be different in the United States from what they
are in Japan, where there seems to be a more fundamental lack of
confidence in the political system.

In Japan, the sudden collapse in 1993 of the Liberal Democratic party
(LDP) that had ruled Japan continuously since 1955 has made the country's politics much less predictable. The LDP had presided over Japan's
postwar recovery and rapid economic growth. During the period of
uninterrupted LDP rule, people in Japan tolerated a series of scandals
in large measure because no opposition party or individual of significant
stature existed to mount a challenge. After promises of political reform

TABLE 5–19
DECLINE IN SUPPORT FOR THE LIBERAL DEMOCRATIC PARTY IN JAPAN,
1961–1995
(percent)

Question: Which political party do you support?

	Jiji		Asahi		Yomiuri	
	LDP	None	LDP	None	LDP	None
1961	39	7	—	—	—	—
1962	40	8	—	—	—	—
1963	38	12	—	—	—	—
1964	39	11	—	—	—	—
1965	40	14	—	—	—	—
1966	39	11	—	—	—	—
1967	34	11	—	—	—	—
1968	38	15	—	—	—	—
1969	33	15	—	—	—	—
1970	41	16	—	—	—	—
1971	33	18	—	—	—	—
1972	29	22	—	—	—	—
1973	32	20	—	—	—	—
1974	24	25	—	—	—	—
1975	24	29	—	—	—	—
1976	26	30	—	—	—	—
1977	29	30	—	—	—	—
1978	32	28	—	—	—	—
1979	32	32	46	5	42	29
1980	30	31	55	4	46	26
1981	33	32	53	5	46	25
1982	30	33	53	6	43	30
1983	30	33	48	5	45	24
1984	34	29	55	6	47	26
1985	34	34	57	6	52	27
1986	32	34	55	5	53	20
1987	33	36	58	5	46	26
1988	35	34	50	7	47	29
1989	31	38	48	5	33	37
1990	30	34	57	4	50	24
1991	38	30	60	5	53	24
1992	40	31	49	7	46	31
1993	34	35	32	9	37	37
1994	22	37	36	16	27	43
1995	21	60	43	42	27	50

NOTES: Jiji Press data are from January of each year except 1995. Data for
1995 are from December. The Asahi data are from December of each year,

(notes continue)

135

from LDP Premier Kiichi Miyazawa were not kept, a reform-oriented faction of the party joined with other opposition members, and a vote of no confidence toppled the Miyazawa government. Mirohito Hosokawa (a former LDP member and founder of the Japan New party) came to power, styling himself as a political reformer. Hosokawa enjoyed high approval ratings for most of his eight-month tenure in office, though reform proved difficult for him, too. He resigned under a cloud after eight months. Tsutomo Hata succeeded Hosokawa for a brief two months. Tomiichi Murayama, the former head of Japan's Socialist party (now the Social Democratic party [SDP] of Japan), then presided until January 11, 1996. On January 12, LDP leader Ryutaro Hashimoto became Japan's sixth prime minister in as many years. Hashimoto will lead the same fragile three-member coalition that Murayama headed until the next parliamentary election—a vote that could take place any time before the summer of 1997. The current makeup of Japan's 511-seat lower house includes 207 LDP members, 63 SDP members, 22 from Sakigake, 170 from Shinshinto, 15 from the Japan Communist party (JCP), 20 from other parties (and 14 vacancies). The membership of the 252-member upper house is 111 LDP, 39 SDP, 3 Sakigake, 68 Shinshinto, 14 JCP, and 17 from other parties. The Liberal Democratic party remains the largest single party in Japan's powerful lower house, though loyalty to the party has dipped considerably (table 5–19).

Cleaning up political corruption is a high priority for the Japanese. The persistence of corruption no doubt contributes to the relatively deep concerns we find in Japan over the polity's performance. The Japanese electorate seems estranged from its political system, the American electorate merely out of sorts—though many in both countries complain about performance. The United States has been immersed in the enterprise of democracy for considerably longer than has Japan, and it is not surprising that the American polity is more "settled."

except for 1981. Data for 1981 are from March. The *Asahi* results are a combination of responses to two questions. The first asks people which party they like. The second asks which party they support. The *Yomiuri* data are from June or July of each year, except for 1981 (March) and 1995 (December). In December 1995, in the Jiji press data, the Japan Socialist party (JSP) had the support of 6 percent of those surveyed, the New Frontier party 6 percent. In the *Asahi* data, the JSP had the support of 13 percent, the New Frontier party, 18 percent. In the *Yomiuri* data, the JSP had the support of 8 percent, the New Frontier Party of 11 percent.
SOURCE: Surveys by Jiji Press, the *Asahi Shimbun*, and the *Yomiuri Shimbun*, latest that of December 1995.

CHAPTER 6

America and Japan—
Similar and Different

By now, the reader has a sense of the extraordinary amount of survey data that exist on life in America and Japan. The Japanese data discussed here represent only a small part of the substantial and growing collection of attitudinal data that the Roper Center at the University of Connecticut will soon make available to researchers. As we said in the introduction, we see this book as a starting point for others. We hope that it will encourage researchers to delve more deeply into the Roper Center collection.

After reviewing thousands of survey questions, we give the polling organizations high marks for their efforts. We do have one complaint that applies mostly to the media-polling partnerships. Pollsters in these relationships tend to poll during "crisis" periods, a practice driven by the competitive instincts of the modern media. Polls are conducted when tempers are running high and differences between the two nations may be exaggerated. Issues are not revisited until the next crisis, when public feelings may again have reached an unnatural intensity. We believe that a subject as important as U.S.-Japanese relations is worthy of regular, sustained attention. This said, the media polls and the many others reviewed here have provided extensive information about our two societies, from which we can draw some general conclusions.

In the area of military and diplomatic relations, the data suggest that significantly different views on the use of military force will continue to produce friction. Still, there is much goodwill in this sphere. Trade issues are not the first concerns people think about when they wake up in the morning, and it is worth noting that some economic tempests of the past—fear of Japanese investment in the United States, for example—have disappeared from the polls and from politicians' agendas, and "crises" have been weathered. Still, economic tensions evident in the surveys cannot be ignored. Americans are now more likely than in the past to see the Japanese government as intransigent.

Extensive cross-national comparisons ultimately present the analyst with something of a quandary. He or she inevitably finds differences between the two countries, which at least in some areas are substantial. But he or she finds significant similarities. The issue is: which—the similarities or the differences—predominate? Which are the more remarkable?

A massive assemblage of literature, both popular and academic, on the United States and Japan, argues a variant of "east is east and west is west. . . ." America and Japan are portrayed as vastly different social systems, animated by sharply contrasting values. It is often said that the Japanese have not embraced (and perhaps never will embrace) the central assumptions of individualism that are so dear to Americans. At the time we began reviewing Japanese survey findings three years ago, we were prepared to accept at least a substantial part of this argument. Now, as we conclude the book, we reject it.

The Study of the "Japanese National Character"

In September 1995, the Institute of Statistical Mathematics released the results of its ninth survey of Japanese values.[1] This latest study was taken in 1993, continuing an every-five-year examination that was launched in 1953. The work is exceptionally good—a model of effective research on national values.

Reviewing the findings of this comprehensive survey, we see broad areas—including several where much of the literature stresses inter-country differences—where the Japanese in fact respond much as Americans would, and indeed have, when comparable questions were posed to them (table 6–1).

The institute asked, "What single thing do you think is the most important in life?" without offering any preset answer-category options. Respondents replied with variants of "family" and "children" far more frequently than anything else, including "happiness" or "health." Americans do this, too. A related set of questions in the

---

1. Yosiyuki Sakamoto et al., "A Study of the Japanese National Character: Ninth Nationwide Survey," Institute of Statistical Mathematics, September 1995.

TABLE 6–1
The Central Values Held by the Japanese, 1993
(percent)

1. Question: What single thing do you think is the most important in life? (open-end)

Family	42
Health	17
Happiness	14
Child	10
Other	9
Wealth	4

2-3. Question: Using this scale, where "7" is *very important,* and "1" is *not important at all,* can you tell me how important each of the following is to you?

First of all, how about your immediate family and children if you have any?

	Scale	Percent
Not important at all	1	1
	2	1
	3	1
	4	4
	5	8
	6	10
Very important	7	75

How about career and work?		
Not important at all	1	1
	2	1
	3	4
	4	14
	5	18
	6	21
Very important	7	37

(table continues)

TABLE 6–1 (continued)

4. Question: Suppose that a child comes home and says that he has heard a rumor that his teacher had done something to get himself into trouble, and suppose that the parent knows this is true. Do you think it is better for the parent to tell the child that it is true, or to deny it?

Better to affirm	59
Better to deny	24

5. Question: Suppose that you were the president of a company. The company decides to employ one person, and then carries out an employment examination. The supervisor in charge reports to you, saying, "Your relative who took the examination got the second highest grade. But I believe that either your relative or the candidate who got the highest grade would be satisfactory. What shall we do?"

Employ one with the highest grade	67
Employ your relative	24

6. Question: A certain department in a firm, having canvassed opinions as to what they should do for their regular outing, decides to go on a two-day trip. Supposing one of the employees doesn't like such trips and had suggested something else. What should he do? (1988)

No need to go if he doesn't enjoy such outings	52
He ought to go even if he doesn't enjoy them	45

7. Question: When a company decides on salaries and wages, do you think that they should attach greatest importance to a person's current abilities in making the decision? Or do you think the person's service to the company from past to present should be stressed in the decision?

They should stress the person's current abilities in deciding	59
They should stress the person's service to the company from past to present in deciding	30

TABLE 6–1 (continued)

8. Question: If you look at the successful people in society today, which do you think has played the largest part in their success: their ability and effort, or luck and chance?

Ability and effort	52
Luck and chance	35

9. Question: Do you think you can put your trust in most people, or do you think it's always best to be on your guard?

People can be trusted	38
Always best to be on your guard	55

10. Question: Do you think that other people are always out to make use of you if ever they see an opportunity, or do you think that's not true?

Not true	65
They are out to make use of you	25

SOURCE: Survey by the Institute for Statistical Mathematics (Japan), 1993.

institute survey asks how important are certain dimensions of life. As we see in table 6–1, three-quarters of the Japanese put "family and children" in position 7 (the most important); only 37 percent assigned this high rank to work and career. Again, many surveys show that Americans set the same priorities. They also show that when people care deeply about these values, they worry about their deterioration. The CBS News/*New York Times*/Tokyo Broadcasting System poll taken in February 1989 after Emperor Hirohito's death found that people in Japan and the United States felt that the younger generation was not as committed to traditional values as was its parents' generation. Both thought the younger generation did not work as hard as its elders.

We see in both countries concern about whether our children will have a better life than we have. Many polls confirm these natural concerns. We agree that we enjoy a better life than our parents did. The March 1995 *Wall Street Journal/Nihon Keizai Shimbun* survey found that 64 percent in the United States and 73 percent in Japan say their generation is enjoying a higher standard of living than did their parents' generation. So on these broad and important values, the Japanese and the Americans seem very much alike.

Other questions in the institute's survey measure the extent to which Japanese respond positively to an individualist model of society and all that it entails. Individualist societies are inherently competitive, as individuals seek personal advancement inevitably in part at the expense of others. The fourth question reported in table 6–1 seeks to determine how strong the older impulses—for a more cooperative and nonconfrontational system—still are, by looking at the norms imparted in child-rearing. Nearly 60 percent of respondents in the 1993 survey said that parents should "tell it like it is" when a child presents them with a well-founded rumor about a teacher, even if doing so roils the waters. When the institute began asking this question in 1953, the "better to affirm" response was chosen by just 42 percent of respondents, 17 points lower than in 1993. Parents were then more concerned with the preservation of their children's respect for an authority figure, even where it may not have been deserved.

The fifth question in the table addresses a facet of competitive individualism more directly. If your company can hire just one person, and it uses a competitive examination to select that person, and a relative of yours gets the second-highest grade—one that shows him to be well-suited to the post—should the job go to the individual who had *the highest* grade, or to your second-place kinsman? By better than two to one, Japanese respondents said—"follow individual merit." Americans answer this kind of question in much the same way. Questions 6 and 7 in the table show other consistent responses. For example, a majority say that if an individual does not want to go on a regular outing his company is sponsoring, he should not go. In a companion question not shown here, respondents also say that although they believe the individual *should not go,* most people in fact *would go.* Nonetheless, the stated norm posits individual assertiveness. In the seventh question, Japanese respondents by two to one declare themselves in favor of companies' rewarding current individual performance rather than past service. Asked (question 8) whether people get ahead through their own effort and ability or through luck, a growing plurality of Japanese say it is individual effort that decides. Even more Americans take this position—in surveys done annually by the National Opinion Research Center.

The last two questions in table 6–1 seek to measure the degree of cynicism, or optimism, about the behavior and motives of one's fellow citizens. Asked (question 9) whether you can place your trust in most people, or if it is best to be "on your guard," Japanese respondents by a substantial majority say "be on guard." But asked whether other people are always out to use you when they can get away with it, they reject such a cynical view by an overwhelming margin. Americans make the same distinction. Indeed, it is very much part of the popular image of Uncle Sam that he's got his guard up, but he is hardly despairing of the human condition.

Together, these responses seem to us a quite remarkable demonstration of the extent to which the two societies—though they have had very different historical experience—have in their postindustrial eras moved relatively close together on many social values involving the status of the individual. Those looking for evidence that the two nations' values are becoming "the same" won't find it. But if instead the issue is whether they display growing similarities, the answer in our judgment is an emphatic "yes."

Areas of Convergence, and Continuing Divergence

Not surprisingly, Americans and Japanese differ more on some questions than on others. We get a further sense of these distinctions when we compare the responses by age in each country—of the youngest adult generation (persons now eighteen–twenty-nine years of age) and the oldest (those who came of age before World War II, during the war, or just after it). Some age-group comparisons were shown in chapter 5 (tables 5–2 through 5–5, 5–13, and 5–16). Here we present additional age-group responses, drawing on survey work taken in the United States and Japan in 1993 and 1994 as part of the International Social Survey Programme.

In a broad array of social values—attitudes toward work and leisure, gender relations, norms for sexual conduct, and the like—convergence between Americans and Japanese is the most striking (table 6–2). On many of these questions we see significantly smaller differences between the young of the two countries than between the old. These values often comprise areas where the societies are changing their mind, departing from historic assumptions and practices. As is typically the case when significant value change is occurring, the young lead the way. And here they are adopting positions closer to each other's than to those of their elders.

On these questions as on so many reviewed in this volume, Japanese of all ages are more inclined than Americans to take the middle ground. The questions shown in table 6–2 all invite, along with "agree"

TABLE 6–2
AMERICAN AND JAPANESE SOCIAL VALUES, 1994
(percent)

Question: How much do you agree or disagree with each of these statements—strongly agree, agree, neither agree nor disagree, disagree, or strongly disagree?

A man's job is to earn money, a woman's job is to look after the home and family.

	18–29 years	60–69 years	70+ years
Agree			
Americans	13	28	47
Japanese	29	61	69
Disagree			
Americans	72	48	30
Japanese	47	22	14

It is not good if the man stays at home and cares for the children and the woman goes out to work.

Agree			
Americans	16	33	46
Japanese	26	60	60
Disagree			
Americans	64	42	33
Japanese	48	29	21

A job is all right, but what most women really want is a home and children.

Agree			
Americans	22	38	62
Japanese	28	63	78
Disagree			
Americans	53	35	14
Japanese	31	17	11

TABLE 6–2 (continued)

When there are children in the family, parents should stay together even if they don't get along.

	18–29 years	60–69 years	70+ years
Agree			
Americans	15	17	25
Japanese	53	77	85
Disagree			
Americans	64	62	50
Japanese	15	13	5

It is all right for a couple to live together without intending to get married.

	18–29 years	60–69 years	70+ years
Agree			
Americans	57	19	9
Japanese	53	25	19
Disagree			
Americans	28	59	76
Japanese	17	62	63

Question: Do you think it is wrong or not wrong if a man and a woman have sexual relations before marriage?

	18–29 years	60–69 years	70+ years
Wrong			
Americans	24	55	69
Japanese	13	70	81
Not Wrong			
Americans	70	37	20
Japanese	82	24	14

SOURCE: Survey by the International Social Survey Programme, 1994.

and "disagree" responses, that of "neither agree nor disagree." The often-larger proportion of Japanese choosing this intermediate response somewhat complicates comparison of the "agree"/"disagree" proportions. Still, the gap between those young Americans and those young Japanese accepting, for example, the old order in gender relations is generally smaller than that between those who are in their sixties and older. Asked whether they agree that "it is not good if the man

145

stays at home and cares for the children and the woman goes out to work," 60 percent of Japanese sixty years old and older say it is not good, compared with just 26 percent of those eighteen to twenty-nine years old. In the United States there is a similar progression of opinion from the oldest to the youngest, but young and old Americans differ less than do their Japanese counterparts (table 6–2).

On many political questions, however, such as role-of-government issues, we see sharp inter-country differences. We also see less evidence of even modest convergence when we compare the youngest respondents. As noted in chapter 5, the Japanese are more inclined than Americans to look to the state for answers, to assign it primary responsibility in meeting perceived problems. These differences show little sign of declining, when one compares the gap between young peoples' answers with that between the elderly (table 6–3 and table 5–13). Relatedly, while Japanese citizens express deeper concern about the environment than do Americans, when asked whether they have joined groups formed to protect the environment, or have given money to such groups, Japanese of all ages are much less likely than Americans to have done either (table 6–3).

While there are certainly exceptions, inter-country differences seem to be diminishing on many social issues. We see this in the fact that young people generally differ less than their elders. At the same time, sharp differences continue on many political questions, especially those involving the role of government, and on taking individual action to advance political ends. What accounts for this pattern? We suspect the answer lies in the fact that powerful structural forces are encouraging convergence in the one sector far more than in the other. The socioeconomy of postindustrialism strongly promotes the assertion of individual claims—of young women, for example, to make their way in the work force and to escape what has come to be seen as excessive burdens in child rearing. At the same time, communications media in both America and Japan constantly reinforce the newer norms on these social issues. Thus the economy encourages new gender relations, to take a specific example, and the mass media in both countries implicitly endorse them. The powerful force of a global popular culture has an immediate impact on social values and lifestyles and brings the young closer together.

The same dynamic does not operate on many of the political issues, however. While there are signs cross-nationally that governmental solutions find less favor now than in earlier periods, America's pervasive "nonstatism" is not being replicated in Japan or, for

TABLE 6–3
THE INDIVIDUALIST NORM AND POLITICAL INCLINATIONS, 1993
(percent)

Question: How much do you agree or disagree with each of these statements—strongly agree, agree, neither agree nor disagree, disagree, or strongly disagree?

It is the responsibility of the government to reduce the differences in income between people with high incomes and those with low incomes.

	18–29 years	60–69 years	70+ years
Agree			
Americans	37	31	29
Japanese	52	56	57
Disagree			
Americans	36	59	46
Japanese	11	17	14

Private enterprise is the best way to solve America's economic problems.

	18–29 years	60–69 years	70+ years
Agreel			
Americans	35	59	69
Japanese	8	13	19
Disagree			
Americans	21	11	9
Japanese	51	43	35

Economic growth always harms the environment.

	18–29 years	60–69 years	70+ years
Agree			
Americans	24	17	26
Japanese	55	66	45
Disagree			
Americans	52	53	46
Japanese	16	10	13

(table continues)

TABLE 6–3 (continued)

Question: In the past five years, have you . . . given money to an environmental group?

	18–29 years	60–69 years	70+ years
Yes			
Americans	62	79	72
Japanese	7	10	6
No			
Americans	38	21	28
Japanese	93	90	94

Question: Are you a member of any group whose main aim is to preserve or protect the environment?

	18–29 years	60–69 years	70+ years
Yes			
Americans	11	11	5
Japanese	1	5	1
No			
Americans	89	89	95
Japanese	99	95	99

SOURCE: Survey by the International Social Survey Programme, 1993.

that matter, across Western Europe. Neither the socioeconomy of postindustrialism nor the influence of the mass media generates nearly the same magnitude of change on the political questions as each does on a wide sweep of social values.

Even in social values, we see areas where sharp differences persist between Americans and Japanese. This is especially evident in religious beliefs. Nonetheless, we see abundant evidence in support of Alexis de Tocqueville's grand hypothesis. The social outlook of Americans and Japanese is becoming less dissimilar. This move toward convergence centers around the spread of individualist norms and assumptions—encouraged by the spread of a global popular culture and by the greater opportunities for individual expression that postindustrial affluence makes possible.

Appendix

TABLE A–1
GROSS DOMESTIC PRODUCT IN PURCHASING POWER PARITIES, 1970–1993
(in billions of dollars)

	United States	Japan	OECD Average
1970	4,933	2,829	3,328
1971	5,288	3,083	3,588
1972	5,755	3,458	3,915
1973	6,373	3,869	4,358
1974	6,830	4,131	4,740
1975	7,351	4,608	5,150
1976	8,120	5,052	5,684
1977	8,969	5,592	6,233
1978	10,017	6,257	6,920
1979	11,046	7,124	7,723
1980	11,891	8,011	8,464
1981	13,191	9,036	9,373
1982	13,558	9,826	9,850
1983	14,456	10,416	10,401
1984	15,879	11,218	11,217
1985	16,786	12,112	11,888
1986	17,510	12,662	12,409
1987	18,433	13,524	13,109
1988	19,707	14,854	14,072
1989	20,920	16,168	15,036
1990	21,965	17,596	15,946
1991	22,385	18,951	16,537
1992	23,228	20,131	17,526
1993	24,302	20,523	17,880

SOURCE: *OECD in Figures*, 1995 edition.

TABLE A–2
THE U.S. TRADE DEFICIT AND THE JAPANESE TRADE SURPLUS, 1982–1993
(billions of dollars)

	United States	*Japan*
1982	−8.64	6.85
1983	−44.31	20.80
1984	−98.99	35.00
1985	−122.25	49.17
1986	−147.54	85.83
1987	−163.45	87.02
1988	−126.67	79.61
1989	−101.19	56.99
1990	−90.46	35.87
1991	−8.32	72.91
1992	−66.38	117.64
1993	−109.25	131.45

SOURCE: *Japan 1995: An International Comparison* (Tokyo, Japan: Keizai Koho Center/Japan Institute for Social and Economic Affairs).

TABLE A–3
MANUFACTURING OUTPUT IN JAPAN AND THE UNITED STATES, 1980–1993

	United States	*Japan*
1980–87 (Index: 1980 = 100)	132	138
1985–90 (Index: 1985 = 100)	120	126
1990–93 (Index: 1990 = 100)	105	91

SOURCE: *OECD in Figures,* 1995 edition.

TABLE A–4
SPENDING FOR R&D AND TECHNOLOGY BALANCE OF PAYMENTS IN THE
UNITED STATES AND JAPAN
(dollars)

	United States	Japan
Per capita expenditure for R&D (in purchasing power parities)[a]	653	588
Technological balance of payments (in millions of $, at official exchange rates)[b]		
Receipts	19,922	2,982
Payments	4,987	3,268
Balance	14,935	−286

a. The OECD indicates that Japan R&D expenditures are overstated in the data; those of the United States are understated.
b. The term refers to imports and exports of high-technology products.
SOURCE: *OECD in Figures*, 1995 edition. Data are most currently available from source.

TABLE A–5
SPENDING FOR EDUCATION IN THE UNITED STATES, JAPAN, AND SIX OTHER OECD COUNTRIES
(millions of dollars)

Country	Per Capita for Higher Education ($)	Per Capita for Primary and Secondary ($)	Full-time Students Enrolled in Higher Education (per 1,000 population)	Percent of 20–24 Year-Olds (per 1,000 of age-group population)
United States	13,890	6,010	32	65
Japan	7,140	3,710	27	53
Canada	11,880	NA	NA	NA
France	5,760	4,600	32	48
Germany	6,550	3,860	28	48
Italy	5,850	4,470	27	42
United Kingdom	10,370	3,780	15	37
Sweden	7,120	5,450	NA	NA

SOURCE: For expenditure data, *Education at a Glance*, OECD Indicators, 1995 edition. For full-time students enrolled in higher education, *OECD in Figures*, 1995 edition; for proportion data for the United States and Japan, *OECD in Figures*, 1994 edition. Data are most currently available from sources shown.

TABLE A–6
Assorted Demographic Comparisons of the United States and Japan

	United States	Japan
Average daily food consumption[a]		
Daily calories	3,495	2,622
Ratio of starchy foods (%)	23	46
Fat (grams)	176	83
Consumer goods: % of households with[b]		
Refrigerator	80	98
Washing machine	76	100
Vacuum cleaner	NA	99
Color television	96	99
Microwave oven	79	70
Television receivers per 1,000 people[c]	814	613
Radio receivers per 1,000 people	2,118	907
Daily newspaper circulation per 1,000 people	249	587
Annual energy consumption[d]		
Energy (coal equiv.) per capita (kilograms)	10,798	4,754
Electric energy (bil. kWh)	2,354	578
Life expectancy (years)[e]		
Women	78.9	82.5
Men	71.9	76.3
Distribution of households (%)[f]		
Married-couple households	56	65
Single-parent households	8	2
One-person households	25	23
Other households	11	10
Extended-family-unit households[g]	10	18
Labor force participation rate (%)[h]	66	63
Hours worked per week[i]	42	44
Percentage of population with cars[j]	90	80

(table continues)

TABLE A–6 (continued)

	United States	Japan
Median commute to work (minutes)[k]	22	27

NOTES: NA = not available.
SOURCES: Data are most currently available from sources shown. a. Bureau of Labor Statistics (U.S.); Ministry of Labor (Japan); b. *Statistical Abstract of the United States,* 1995 edition; *Japan 1995: An International Comparison*; c. *Statistical Abstract of the United States,* 1995 edition; d. *Statistical Abstract of the United States,* 1995 edition; e. *Japan 1995: An International Comparison*; f. *Statistical Abstract of the United States,* 1995 edition; g. Embassy of Japan; h. *Statistical Abstract of the United States,* 1995 edition; i. Bureau of Labor Statistics (U.S.); Japanese Embassy; j. U.S. Census Bureau (U.S.); Japanese Embassy; k. U.S. Census Bureau (U.S.); Japanese Embassy.

TABLE A–7
DIVORCE IN THE UNITED STATES AND JAPAN, 1994
(percent)

Questions: Are you currently married, widowed, divorced, separated, or have you never been married? [If currently married or widowed] have you ever been divorced or legally separated?[a]

Americans	
Currently married/never divorced	51
Divorced at any time/legally separated	29
Never married	21

Question: Have you ever been divorced?

Japanese	
No[b]	74
Never married	23
Yes	4

NOTE: Percentages may not add to 100 because of rounding.
a. Responses to the two NORC questions were combined to provide an equal base to compare with the Japan question.
b. Many Japanese seem reluctant to tell interviewers that they have been divorced, so survey data understate the actual incidence of divorce.
SOURCE: Surveys of the National Opinion Research Center (U.S.), January–May 1994 and NHK Broadcasting Research (Japan), January 1994.

TABLE A–8
NUMBERS OF MARRIAGES AND DIVORCES
IN THE UNITED STATES AND JAPAN

	Marriages	Divorces	Ratio of Divorces to Marriages (percent)
United States	2,362,000	1,215,000	51
Japan	782,735	195,115	25

SOURCE: For the United States, *Statistical Abstract of the United States*, 1995 edition. For Japan, Japan Ministry of Health and Welfare. Data are most currently available from sources shown.

TABLE A–9
IDEAL NUMBER OF CHILDREN IN FAMILIES, IN JAPAN AND THE UNITED STATES
(percent)

Question: What do you think is the ideal size of the family—how many children, if any?

Number of Children	Americans	Japanese
0	2	a
1	3	1
2	47	34
3	23	48
4	13	5
5	3	1
6 or more	2	1

Question: Have you had any children? If yes, how many?

Number of Children	Americans	Japanese
0	28	23
1	14	12
2	25	43
3	15	17
4	9	3
5	5	a
6 or more	4	a

NOTE: Percentages may not add to 100 because of rounding.
a. Less than 1%.
SOURCE: World Values Survey, 1990–1993, conducted by the World Values Study Group.

TABLE A–10
POPULATION INCREASE IN THE UNITED STATES AND JAPAN, 1945–1993
(percent)

Year	United States	Japan
1945 base population	140,468,000	72,147,000
1950	8.4	15.3
1960	28.6	29.5
1970	46.0	43.8
1980	62.1	62.3
1990	77.9	71.3
1993 population	258,245,000	124,764,000
% increase 1945–1993	83.8	72.9

SOURCE: For United States, 1945—*Statistical Abstract of the United States,* 1972 edition; *Statistical Abstract of the United States,* 1994 edition. For Japan, Bureau of Statistics, Management and Coordination Agency.

TABLE A–11
POPULATION BY AGE GROUP IN THE
UNITED STATES AND JAPAN, 1970 AND 1993
(percent)

	United States		Japan	
	1970	1993	1970	1993
0–14 years of age	29	22	24	17
15–64 years of age	62	65	69	70
65+ years of age	10	13	7	14

NOTE: Percentages may not add to 100 because of rounding.
SOURCE: For the United States, *Statistical Abstract of the United States,* 1994 edition. For Japan, Bureau of Statistics, Management and Coordination Agency.

TABLE A-12
HEALTH CARE SPENDING IN THE UNITED STATES, JAPAN, AND ELEVEN OTHER OECD COUNTRIES, 1983 AND 1993

	As % of GDP		Per Capita GDP in $ PPPs	
	1983	1993	1983	1993
United States	11	14	1,489	3,299
Japan	7	7	719	1,495
Canada	9	10	1,040	1,971
Denmark	7	7	729	1,276
France	8	10	954	1,835
Germany	9	9	1,012	1,814
Italy	7	9	729	1,523
Netherlands	8	8	869	1,532
Norway	7	8	726	1,592
Spain	6	7	433	972
Sweden	10	8	1,094	1,266
Switzerland	8	10	1,116	2,283
United Kingdom	6	7	605	1,213

SOURCE: *OECD in Figures,* 1995 edition.

TABLE A–13
TAXES IN THE UNITED STATES, JAPAN, AND ELEVEN OTHER OECD COUNTRIES
(percent)

	Total Taxes as % of GDP	Taxes on Goods and Services	Highest Rate of Central Government Personal Income Tax
United States	29	17	31
Japan	29	14	50
Canada	37	26	29
Denmark	49	33	40
France	44	27	57
Germany	40	27	53
Italy	42	27	51
Netherlands	47	26	60
Norway	47	37	13
Spain	36	29	56
Sweden	50	27	20
Switzerland	32	17	13
United Kingdom	35	34	40

SOURCE: *OECD in Figures*, 1995 edition. Data are most currently available from source.

TABLE A–14
DEFENSE OUTLAYS IN THE UNITED STATES, JAPAN, AND FIVE OTHER OECD COUNTRIES

	$ Expenditures, Per Capita	Ratio to GNP
United States	1,222	5.3
Japan	288	0.9
Canada	415	2.0
France	754	3.4
Germany	531	2.4
Italy	425	2.0
United Kingdom	724	4.0

SOURCE: *Japan 1995: An International Comparison* (Tokyo, Japan: Keizai Koho Center/Japan Institute for Social and Economic Affairs). Data are most currently available from sources.

About the Authors

EVERETT CARLL LADD is the director of the Institute for Social Inquiry at the University of Connecticut. He is also the executive director and president of the Roper Center for Public Opinion Research, a private, nonprofit research facility affiliated with the University of Connecticut since 1977.

Mr. Ladd's principal research interests are American political thought, public opinion, and political parties. Among his ten books are *American Political Parties: Ideology in America; Transformations of the American Party System; Where Have All the Voters Gone?* and *The American Polity* (all published by W.W. Norton).

An AEI adjunct scholar, he is a contributor to *The Standard,* a member of the editorial boards of four magazines, and the editor of the Roper Center's magazine, *Public Perspective.* In recent years, he has been a fellow of the Ford, Guggenheim, and Rockefeller Foundations; the Center for International Studies at Harvard; the Hoover Institution at Stanford; and the Center for Advanced Study in the Behavioral Sciences.

KARLYN H. BOWMAN is a resident fellow at the American Enterprise Institute. She joined AEI in 1979, and was managing editor of *Public Opinion* until 1990. From 1990 to 1995 she was the editor of *The American Enterprise.* Ms. Bowman continues as editor of the magazine's "Opinion Pulse" section, and she writes about public opinion and demographics. Her most recent publications include "Public Attitudes toward the People's Republic of China," in *Beyond MFN: Trade with China and American Interests* (AEI Press, 1994); "Public Opinion toward Congress" (with Everett Carll Ladd), in *Congress, the Press, and the Public* (AEI-Brookings, 1994); and *The 1993–1994 Debate on Health Care Reform: Did the Polls Mislead the Policy Makers?* (AEI Press, 1994).

A Note on the Book

*This book was edited by Cheryl Weissman
and Dana Lane
of the publications staff
of the American Enterprise Institute.
The text was set in New Baskerville.
Publication Technology Corporation of Fairfax, Virginia,
set the type, and Data Reproductions Corporation,
of Rochester Hills, Michigan, using permanent acid-free paper,
printed and bound the book.*

The AEI Press is the publisher for the American Enterprise Institute for Public Policy Research, 1150 17th Street, N.W., Washington, D.C. 20036; *Christopher C. DeMuth,* publisher; *Dana Lane,* director; *Ann Petty,* editor; *Leigh Tripoli,* editor; *Cheryl Weissman,* editor; *Lisa Roman,* editorial assistant (rights and permissions).